THE

THE VEIL OF ISIS;

OR,

MYSTERIES OF THE DRUIDS

BY

W. WINWOOD READE.

" By the bright circle of the golden sun,
  By the bright courses of the errant moon,
  By the dread potency of every star,
  In the mysterious Zodiac's burning girth,
  By each and all of these supernal signs,
  We do adjure thee, with this trusty blade
  To guard yon central oak, whose holy stem,
  Involves the spirit of high Taranis:
  Be this thy charge."—MASON.

―――――

NEWCASTLE PUBLISHING COMPANY INC.
North Hollywood, California
1992

DEDICATION.

TO EMILY * * *.

As those presents are always the most fashionable, and sometimes the most valued, which cannot be used, I give you this book, which you will not be able to read, but which, perhaps, you will kindly preserve in memory of its writer.

An author can pay no higher compliment to a friend than to dedicate to her a work upon which he has spent much labor and anxiety. This effort of a young man to redeem a mistake, perhaps a fault, in his literary life, deserves to be sealed with your name, for it is you who have repeatedly urged him to the task, and presided over it like a guardian angel, with kind and consoling words.

CONTENTS.

BOOK THE FIRST.

DARKNESS.

BOOK THE SECOND.

ABORIGINES.

BOOK THE THIRD.

THE DRUIDS.

5

Contents.

BOOK THE FOURTH.

THE DESTRUCTION OF THE DRUIDS.

BOOK THE FIFTH.

VESTIGES OF DRUIDISM.

APPENDIX.

BOOK THE FIRST.

DARKNESS

THE VEIL OF ISIS;

OR,

THE MYSTERIES OF THE DRUIDS.

THERE is no study so saddening, and none so sublime as that of the early religions of mankind. To trace back the worship of God to its simple origin, and to mark the gradual process of those degrading superstitions, and unhallowed rites which darkened, and finally extinguished His presence in the ancient world.

At first men enjoyed the blessings of nature as children do, without inquiring into causes. It was sufficient for them that the earth gave them herbs, that the trees bore them fruit, that the stream quenched their thirst. They were happy, and every moment though unconsciously they offered a prayer of gratitude to Him whom as yet they did not know.

And then a system of theology arose amongst them vague and indefinite, as the waters of the boundless sea. They taught each other that the sun, and

9

the earth, the moon, and the stars were moved and illumined by a Great Soul which was the source of all life, which caused the birds to sing, the brooks to murmur, and the sea to heave. It was a sacred Fire which shone in the firmament, and in mighty flames. It was a strange Being which animated the souls of men, and which when the bodies died, returned to itself again.

They silently adored this Great Soul in the beginning, and spoke of Him with reverence, and sometimes raised their eyes timidly to His glittering dwelling-place on high.

And soon they learned to pray. When those whom they loved lay dying, they uttered wild lamentations, and flung their arms despairingly towards the mysterious Soul; for in times of trouble the human mind so imbecile, so helpless, clings to something that is stronger than itself.

As yet they worshipped only the sun, the moon, and the stars—and not as Gods but as visions of that Divine Essence, which alone ruled and pervaded the earth, the sky, and the sea.

They adored Him kneeling, with their hands clasped, and their eyes raised. They offered Him no sacrifices, they built Him no temples; they were content to offer Him their hearts which were full of awe, in His own temple which was full of grandeur.

And it is said that there are yet some barbarous islands where men have no churches nor ceremonies, and where they worship God, reflected in the work of His thousand hands.

But they were not long content with this simple service. Prayer which had first been an inspiration fell into a system, and men already grown wicked prayed the Deity to give them abundance of wild beast's skins, and to destroy their enemies.

They ascended eminences, as if hoping that thus being nearer God, He would prefer their prayers to those of their rivals. Such is the origin of that superstitious reverence for high places which was universal throughout the whole of the heathen world.

Then Orpheus was born. And he invented instruments which to his touch and to his lips, gave forth notes of surpassing sweetness, and with these melodies he enticed the wondering savages into the recesses of the forest, and there taught them precepts of obedience to the great Soul, and of loving-kindness towards each other in harmonious words.

So they devoted groves and forests to the worship of the Deity.

There were men who had watched Orpheus, and who had seen and envied his power over the herd who surrounded him. They resolved to imitate him, and having studied these barbarians, they banded together, and called themselves their priests. Religion ·is divine, but its ministers are men. And alas! sometimes they are demons with the faces and wings of angels.

The simplicity of men, and the cunning of their priests has destroyed or corrupted all the religions of the world.

These priests taught the people to sacrifice the choicest herbs and flowers. They taught them formulas of prayer, and bade them make so many obeisances to the sun, and to worship those flowers which opened their leaves when he rose, and which closed them as he set.

They composed a language of symbols which was perhaps necessary, since letters had not been invented, but which perplexed the people and perverted them from the worship of the one God.

Thus the sun and moon were worshipped as emblems of God, and fire as an emblem of the sun, water as an emblem of the moon.

The serpent was to be worshipped also as an emblem of wisdom and eternal youth, since it renews its skin every year, and thus periodically casts off all symptoms of old age.

And the bull, most vigorous of animals, and whose horns resemble those of the crescent moon.

The priests observed the avidity with which the

barbarians adored these symbols, and increased them. To worship the visible is a disease of the soul inherent to all mankind, and the disease which these men could have healed they pandered to.

It is true that the first generation of men might have looked upon these merely as the empty symbols of a Divine Being, but it is also certain that in time the vulgar forgot the God in the emblem, and worshipped that which their fathers had only honored. Egypt was the fountain-head of these idolatries, and it was in Egypt that the priests first applied real attributes to the sun, and to the moon whom they called his wife.

It may perhaps interest you to listen to the first fable of the world.

From the midst of chaos was born Osiris, and at his birth a voice was heard proclaiming—" *The ruler of all the earth is born.*"

From the same dark and troubled womb were born Isis the Queen of Light, and Typhon the Spirit of Darkness.

This Osiris traveled over the whole world, and civilized its inhabitants, and taught them the art of agriculture. But on his return to Egypt the jealous Typhon laid a stratagem for him, and in the midst of a banquet had him shut up in a chest which exactly fitted his body. He was nailed down in his prison, which cast into the Nile floated down to the sea by the Taitic mouth, which even in the time of Plutarch was never mentioned by an Egyptian but with marks of detestation.

When Isis learnt these sad new she cut off a lock of her hair, and put on her mourning robes, and wandered through the whole country in search of the chest which contained the dead body of her husband.

At length she learnt that the chest had been carried by the waves to the shore of Byblos, and had there lodged in the branches of a tamarisk bush, which quickly shot up and became a large and beautiful tree, growing round the chest so that it could not be seen.

The king of the country amazed at the vast size the tree had so speedily acquired, ordered it to be cut down to be hewn into a pillar to support the roof of his palace—the chest being still concealed in the trunk.

The voice which had spoken from Heaven at the birth of Osiris made known these things to poor Isis, who went to the shore of Byblos and sat down silently by a fountain to weep. The damsels of the queen met her and accosted her, and the queen appointed her to be nurse to her child. And Isis fed the infant with her finger instead of with her breast, and put him every night into fire to render him immortal, while transforming herself into a swallow she hovered round the pillar which was her husband's tomb, and bemoaned her unhappy fate.

It happened that the queen thus discovered her, and shrieked when she saw her child surrounded by flames. By that cry she broke the charm and deprived him of immortality.

By that cry Isis was summoned back to her goddess-form, and stood before the awe-struck queen shining with light and diffusing sweet fragrances around.

She cut open the pillar, and took the coffin with her, and opened it in a desert. There she embraced the cold corpse of Osiris, and wept bitterly.

She returned to Egypt and hid the coffin in a remote place: but Typhon, hunting by moonlight, chanced to find it, and divided the corpse into fourteen pieces. Again Isis set out on her weary search throughout the whole land, sailing over the fenny parts in a boat made of papyrus. She recovered all the fragments except one which had been thrown into the sea. Each of these she buried in the place where she found it, which explains why in Egypt there are so many tombs of Osiris.

And instead of the limb which was lost, she gave the *phallus* to the Egyptians—the disgusting worship of which was thence carried into Italy, into Greece, and into all the countries of the East.

When Isis died, she was buried in a grove near Memphis. Over her grave was raised a statue covered from head to foot with a black veil. And underneath was engraved these divine words:

I am all that has been, that is, that shall be, and none among mortals has yet dared to raise my veil.

Beneath this veil are concealed all the mysteries and learning of the past. A young scholar, his fingers covered with the dust of venerable folios, his eyes weary and reddened by nightly toil will now attempt to lift a corner of this mysterious and sacred covering.

These two Deities, Isis and Osiris were the parents of all the Gods and Godesses of the Heathens, or were indeed those Gods themselves worshipped under different names. The fable itself was received into the mythologies of the Hindoos and the Romans. Sira is said to have mutilated Brahma as Typhon did Osiris, and Venus to have lamented her slain Adonis, as Isis wept for her husband-god.

As yet the sun and moon alone were worshipped under these two names. And as we have seen, besides these twin beneficial spirits, men who had begun to recognize sin in their hearts had created an Evil One who struggled with the power of light, and fought with them for the souls of men.

It is natural for man to fabricate something that

is worse than himself. Even in the theology of the American Indians which is the purest of the modern world, there is found a Mahitou or dark Spirit.

Osiris or the sun was now worshipped throughout the whole world, though under different names. He was the Mithra of the Persians, the Brahma of India, the Baal or Adonis of the Phœnicians, the Apollo of the Greeks, the Odin of Scandinavia, the Hu of the Britons, and the Baiwe of the Laplanders.

Isis also received the names of Islene, Ceres, Rhea, Venus, Vesta, Cybele, Niobe, Melissa—Nehalennia in the North; Isi with the Indians; Puzza among the Chinese; and Ceridwen among the ancient Britons.

The Egyptians were sublime philosophers who had dictated theology to the world. And in Chaldœa arose the first astrologers who watched the heavenly bodies with curiosity as well as with awe, and who made divine discoveries, and who called themselves *The Interpreters of God.*

To each star they gave a name, and to each day in the year they gave a star.

And the Greeks and Romans who were poets, wreathed these names into legends. Each name was a person, each person was a god.

From these stories of the stars originated the angels of the Jews, the genii of the Arabs, the heroes of the Greeks, and the saints of the Romish Church.

Now corruption grew upon corruption, and super-stition flung a black and hideous veil over the doc-trines of religion. A religion is lost as soon as it loses its simplicity: truth has no mysteries: it is deceit alone that lurks in obscurity.

Men multiplied God into a thousand names, and created Him always in their own image. Him, too, whom they had once deemed unworthy of any temple less noble than the floor of the earth and the vast dome of the sky, they worshipped in caves, and then in temples which were made of the trunks of trees rudely sculptured, and ranged in rows to imitate groves, and with other trunks placed upon them traversely.

Such were the first buildings of worship erected by man from no reverence for the Deity, but to display that which they doubtless conceived to be a stupendous effort in art.

It may not be needless to remind some of my readers that a superior being must view the elegant temples of the Romans, the gorgeous pagodas of India, and our own Gothic cathedrals with feelings similar to those with which we contemplate the rude efforts of the early heathens, who deemed God un-worthy of the fruits and flowers which he himself had made, and offered to him the entrails of beasts, and the hearts of human beings.

We may compare an ancient and fallen religion to the ship of the Argonauts, which the Greeks desiring to preserve to posterity, repairing in so many different ways, that at length there did not remain a fragment of that vessel which had born to Colchis the conqueror of the Golden Fleece.

Let us pass over a lapse of years, and then contemplate the condition of these nations in whom religion had been first born. We find the Egyptians adoring the most common of plants, the most contemptible of beasts, the most hideous of reptiles. The solemnity and pomp of their absurd ceremonies held them up to the ridicule of the whole world.

Clemens of Alexandria describes one of their temples:—(Pœdag. lib. iii).—

" The walls shine with gold and silver, and with amber, and sparkle with the gems of India and Ethiopia: and the recesses are concealed by splendid curtains. But if you enter the penetralia, and inquire for the image of God for whose sake the fane was built; one of the Pastophori, or some other attendant on the temple approaches with a solemn and mysterious face, and putting aside the veil suffers you to obtain a glimpse of the divinity. There you behold a snake, a crocodile, or a cat, or some other beast, a fitter inhabitant of a cavern, or a bog than of a temple."

The priests of Egypt, always impostors, but once so celebrated, had now degenerated into a race of jugglers.

Also the Chaldœans lived upon the fame of their fathers, and upon their own base trickeries.

The Brachmans or Brahmins, those priests of India, once so virtuous and so wise—ah! they too had fallen. Once they had forbidden the shedding of so much as an insects blood : one day in the year alone, at the feast of Jagam, they were authorized to sacrifice the flesh of a beast, and from this many had refrained from attending, unable to conquer their feelings of abhorrence.

But now they had learnt from the fierce Scythians and from the Phœnicians who traded on their coasts to sacrifice the wife upon her husbands pyre—to appease the gentle Brahmah with the blood of men.

Now the angels who had presided over them became savage demons, who scourged them on to cruel penances, nay to life-times of suffering and famine.

In the sacred groves where once the Brachman-Fathers had taught their precepts of love, men emaciated, careworn, dying, wandered sadly, waiting for death as tortured prisoners wait for their liberty.

But worse still, these wicked priests sought through the land for the most beautiful young women, and trained them to dance in the temples, and to entice the devotees to their arms with lustful attitudes and languishing looks, and with their voices which mingled harmoniously with the golden bells suspended on their feet.   They sang hymns to the Gods in public, and in private enriched the treasuries of the pagoda with their infamous earnings.   Thus a pure and simple religion was debased by the avarice and lewdness of its priests: till the temples became a den of thieves: till prostitution sat enthroned upon the altars of the Gods.

Greece and Rome buried in sloth and luxury did not escape the general contamination.   The emblem of generation which Isis had bestowed upon the Egyptians, and which they had held in abstract reverence, had now obtained a prominent place in the festivals of these nations as did the Lingam in those of the Hindoos.   It was openly paraded in processions in the streets: it was worn by Roman nations in bracelets upon their arms.

The sacred festivals and mysteries which they had received from the Egyptians, and for which the women had been wont to prepare themselves by continence, and the men by fasting, were now mere vehicles for depravities of the lowest kind.   Men were permitted to join the women in their worship of Bacchus, of Adonis, of the Bona Dea, and even of Priapus, and so dissolute did the Dionusia become, that the civil powers were compelled to interfere with those of religion, and the Bacchanalia were abolished by a decree of the Roman senate.

And the Jews, the chosen people of God, had not their religion changed? had not God, weary with their sins, yielded them to captivity, scourged them with sorrow, menaced them with curses?

They worshipped Baal-peor, the Priapus of Assyria, they sacrificed their children to Moloch: they had dancing-girls in the holy temple.

I will not go deeper into particulars so degrading to human nature. I will rather invite you to follow me to a corner of the world where, at least for many ages religion was preserved in its pristine purity, and whose priests, through a barbarous soldiery, were received as martyrs in heaven before they had learned to be knaves upon earth.

It was an isolated spot unknown to the world in the earlier ages of vice. It is now a kingdom renowned for its power and for its luxuries from hemisphere to hemisphere.

It was encircled by the blue waters of the German and Atlantic Seas, and abounded in the choicest gifts of nature.

It was called *The White Island* from those cliffs which still frown so coldly upon Gaul, and *The Land of Green Hills* from its verdant mountains. Come with me to its shores, and I will show you its priests in their white robes, and its warriors in the blue paint of war, and its virgins with their long and glossy yellow hair.

But first I will lead you back into the past, and relate to you why this land was called Albion, and why Britain.

BOOK THE SECOND.

ABORIGINES.

I.

ALBION.

A S travelers, who have lost their way by night,
gaze ever towards the east for the first rays
of light and hope, so we who grope in the darkness
of antiquity must direct our eyes to the land of the
rising sun, whence learning and life itself first sprang.

Listen then to a romance of the East.

Danaus, King of Greece, had fifty sons, whom he
married to the fifty daughters of his brother Ægistus,
King of Egypt. But soon these women thirsted for
dominion, and conspired secretly to slay their husbands and to rule in their steads. But the youngest
and the most beautiful had a tender heart, which
crept from her lips in words of warning to her father
and her spouse. Then they were all seized and set
adrift in ships upon the sea, which after many storms
bore them in safety to a large and uninhabited
island.

Here they staid and named it Albion, after Albina
their eldest sister, and here they maintained them-

selves by the chase, killing the deer and the boars, and wild bulls, and large birds which they found in the forests with arrows and bolts, and bowstrings, and snares and pitfalls.

And while filled with meat and drink, and with lustful thoughts, they lay sleeping on the ground covered with the skins of wild beasts, dark brooding spirits swept towards them from the sky, and encircled them with their shadowy arms, and intoxicated them with their flaming breath

By these were born huge and hideous giants which soon bore others, till they filled the whole land with a strange and fierce crew.

II.

BRITAIN.

MEANWHILE Troy had fallen: the wanderings of Eneas were past: and Ascanius had died leaving behind him his son Silvius.

The son of Silvius loved a maid, who became pregnant. Then the wise men and women of the land were sent for, and all those who knew songs of magic art. They cast their lots and found sorrowful spells: that a child would be born through whom both his father and mother would suffer death: that through their death he would be driven from the land, and after a long time would be crowned with honor.

His mother died as she gave him to the world, and the child, whom they named Brutus, when he had become a youth, shot his father through the breast a-hunting the deer.

His kindred banished him from the land, and he sailed sadly over the sea-streams into Greece where he headed an insurrection against Pandrasus the

king, and with such success that the king offered
him all his ships, and treasures, and Imogen his
only daughter if he would consent to seek another
kingdom.

So Brutus, with his followers, like Eneas of old,
sailed forth upon the waters in search of a new land.

After two days and two nights the sea became
blue: the wild waves were hushed: they came to a
desolate island: its inhabitants had been slain by the
pirates: the timid deer coursed over its wasted
shores.

But they found there a marble temple, and within
the fair and beautiful image of Diana.

Brutus with twelve wise men, and with Gerion,
his priest, entered the temple while his followers
remained without. He bore a vessel of red gold in
his hand: it was filled with wine and with the milk
of a white hind which he had killed. Having kindled
a fire by the altar, he walked around it nine times.
He called to the goddess beloved of his heart: he
kissed the altar and poured the wine and milk upon
the fire.

"Lady Diana! loved Diana! High Diana!" he
cried. "Help me in my need. Teach me whither
I may go and wherein I may dwell. And there I
will make thee a lofty dwelling and honor thee with
great worship.

Then he spread the hide of the white hind upon
the altar, and kneeling upon it fell asleep. In his
dreams he beheld Diana floating towards him with
sweet smiles. She laid her hands like a wreath of
flowers upon his head, saying :

Beyond Gaul in the west thou shall find a winsome
land: therein thou shalt prosper. Therein is fowl:
there is fish: there dwell fair deer: there is wood:
there is water: there is much desert: grim giants
dwell in the land. It is called *Albion*.

For thirty days and thirty nights they sailed past
Africa and over the lake of Silvius, and over the
lake of Philisteus: by Ruscikadan they took the sea,
and by the mountain country of Azare. They fought
with the pirates, and gained from them such treasures
that there was not a man in the fleet who did not
wear gold and pall. And by the pillars of Hercules
they were encompassed by mermen who sing songs
so sweet that mariners will rest slothfully on their
oars, and listen to them for days without wearying of
their songs to hear—these impeded them much with
their wicked crafts, but they escaped them safely.

In a peaceful sea, and among the playing fish they
came to Dartmouth in Totnes. There the ships
bit the sands, and with merry hearts the warriors
went ashore.

It happened after many days that Brutus and his

people were celebrating holy writs, with meat, with drink, and with merry glee sounds: with silver and with gold: with horses and with vestments.

Twenty strong giants descended the hills: trees were their clubs: in the centre of their foreheads was a single eye vivid as the blue ice. They hurled huge stones and slew five hundred of the Trojans. But soon the fierce steel arrows of the Trojans whistled through the air, and blood began to spurt from their monstrous sides. They tried to fly; but those darts followed them swift and revengeful, as birds of prey winged with the dark feathers of death.

Nineteen were slain and Geog-magog, their leader was brought bound before Brutus, who ordered a wrestling match to be held between the giant and Corineus, a chieftain of his army.

A mighty crowd gathered upon the downs by the sea-cliff.

Corineus and the giant advanced towards each other, they yoked their arms and stood breast to breast. Their eyes gushed blood, their teeth gnashed like wild boars, their bones cracked. Now their faces were black and swollen, now red and flaming with rage. Geog-magog thrust Corineus off his breast and drawing him back broke three of his ribs with his mighty hand. But Corineus was not overcome, he hugged the giant grimly to his waist, and grasping him by the girdle swung him over the cliff upon the rocks below.

Which spot is called "Geog-magog's leap" to this day. And to Corineus, the conqueror, was given a dukedom, which was thence called Corinee and thence Cornwall.

Brutus having conquered the giant off-spring of the treacherous sisters, built a New Troy, and erected temples to the great Diana, and caused her to be worshipped throughout the land.

Which was named *Britain* after Brutus, the first man who set foot upon its shores.

III.

ANALYSIS.

FABLES are seldom actual impostures. They are usually truths disguised in gaudy or grotesque garments, but so disguised that the most profound philosophers are often at a loss how to separate the tinsel from the gold.

But even when they remain insolvable enigmas, they are, at least, to be preferred to the etymological eurekas and tedious conjectures with which antiquarians clog the pages of history, and which are equally false and less poetical.

My fable of Albion is derived from the ancient chronicles of Hugh de Genesis, an historiographer now almost forgotten, and is gravely advanced by John Hardyng, in his uncouth rhymes, as the source of that desire for sovereignty which he affirms to be a peculiarity of his own countrywomen.

The story of Brû or Brutus was first published by Geoffrey of Monmouth, and was generally supposed to have been a monkish fabrication, till it was discovered in the historical poems of Tyssilia, a Welsh bard.

It is worthy of remark that the boys of Wales still amuse themselves by cutting out seven enclosures in the sward, which they call the City of Troy, and dance round and between them as if in imitation of the revolution of the planets.

In a poem by Taliesin, the Ossian of Wales, called *The Appeasing of Lhudd*, a passage occurs, of which this is a literal translation :

"A numerous race, fierce, they are said to have been,
Were thy original colonists, Britain, first of isles,
Natives of a country in Asia, and the city of Gafiz
Said to have been a skilful people, but the district is unknown
Which was mother to these children, warlike adventurers on the sea;
Clad in their long dress, who could equal them?
Their skill is celebrated, they were the dread of Europe."

This is strong evidence in favor of the Phœnicians, at that time the pirate-scourges of the sea, but in the Welsh triads, or traditional chronicles, we read that:—

"*The first of the three chieftains who established the colony was* Hu, *the Mighty, who came with the original settlers. They came over the Hazy Sea from the summer country, which is called* Deffrobani, *that is where* Constinoblys *now stands.*"—Triad 4.

It may be possible to reconcile these contradictions of history in its simplest state, to which I might add a hundred from later writers.

We learn from Josephus that the Scythians were called *Magogæi* by the Greeks, and it is probable that these (who certainly did migrate to Britain at a remote period) were the real aborigines, and the race alluded to in the fourth Triad. That then the warlike race of Taliesin also migrated from another region of the East, and that their battles with the Scythians gave rise to the fables of Brutus and Magog; for it was a practice, common enough with illiterate nations, to express heroes in their war-tales by the images of giants.

This superstition is somewhat borne out by the assertion of Tacitus and other classical writers, that at the time of Cæsar's invasion, there were three distinct races in Britain, especially contrasting—the red-haired, large-limbed, and blue-eyed Celts of the North, with the Silures of Devon, Cornwall, and the Cassiterides or Scilly Isles, who had swarthy faces and dark curly hair, like the Iberi of Spain.

But let us pass on from such dateless periods of guess-work, to that in which *The White Island* first obtained notice from those philosophers, and poets, and historians, whom now we revere and almost deify.

IV.

DESCRIPTION.

THE north of the island was inhabited by wild hordes of savages, who lived upon the bark of trees, and upon the precarious produce of the chase; went naked, and sheltered themselves from the weather under the cover of the woods, or in the mountain caves.

The midland tribes were entirely pastoral. They lived upon the flesh and milk which their flocks afforded them, and clothed themselves in their skins.

While the inhabitants of the south, who had been polished by intercourse with strangers, were acquainted with many of the arts of civilization, and were ruled by a priesthood which was second to none in the world for its learning and experience.

They manured their ground with marl, and sowed corn, which they stored in thatched houses, and from which they took as much as was necessary for the day and having dried the ears, beat the grain out, bruised it, and baked it into bread.

They ate little of this bread at their banquets, but great quantities of flesh, which they either boiled in water, or broiled upon the coals, or roasted upon spits. They drank ale or metheglin, a liquor made of milk and honey, and sat upon the skins of wolves or dogs.

They lived in small houses built in a circular form, thatched with rushes into the shape of a cone; an aperture being left by which the smoke might escape.

Their dress was of their own manufacture. A square mantle covered a vest and trousers, or a deeply-plaited tunic of braided cloth; the waist was encircled by a belt, rings adorned the second finger of each hand, and a chain of iron or brass was suspended from the neck. These mantles, at first the only covering of the Britons, were of one color, with long hair on the outside, and were fastened upon the breast by a clasp, with the poorer classes by a thorn.

The heads were covered with caps made of rushes, and their feet with sandals of untanned skin; specimens of which are still to be met with—of the former in Wales, of the latter in the Shetland Isles.

The women wore tunics, wrought and interwoven with various colors, over which was a loose robe of coarser make, secured with brazen buckles. They let their hair flow at freedom, and dyed it yellow like the ladies of ancient Rome; and they wore chains of massive gold about their necks, bracelets upon their arms, rings upon their fingers.

They were skilled in the art of weaving, in which, however, the Gauls had obtained a still greater proficience. The most valuable of their cloths were manufactured of fine wool of different tints, woven chequer-wise, so as to fall into small squares of various colors. They also made a kind of cloth, which, without spinning or weaving, was, when worked up with vinegar, so hard and impenetrable, that it would turn the edge of the sharpest sword.

They were equally famous for their linen, and sailcloths constituted a great part of their trade.

When they had finished the linen in the loom, they had this curious method of bleaching it :

The flax having been whitened before it was sent to the loom, the unspun yarn was placed in a mortar where it was pounded and beaten into water; it was then sent to the weaver, and when it was received from him made into cloth, it was laid upon a large smooth stone, and beaten with broad-headed cudgels, the juice of poppies being mingled with the water.

For scouring cloths, they used a soap invented by themselves, which they made from the fat of animals and the ashes of certain vegetables

Distinct from these southern tribes, were the inhabitants of the Cassiterides, who wore long black garments, and beards falling on each side of their mouths like wings, and who are described by Pliny as "carrying staves with three serpents curling round like Furies in a tragedy."

It is probable that the nudity of the northern nations did not proceed from mere barbarous ignorance. We know that savages are first induced to wear clothing, not from shame, but from vanity; and it was this passion which restrained them from wearing the skins of beasts, or the gaudy clothes of their civilized neighbors.

For it was their custom to adorn their bodies with various figures by a tedious and painful process. At an early age, the outlines of animals were impressed with a pointed instrument into the skin; a strong infusion of *woad*, (a Gallic herb from which a blue dye was extracted) was rubbed into the punctures, and the figures expanding with the growth of the body retained their original appearance. Like the South-Sea Islanders they esteemed that to be a decoration which we consider a disfigurement, and these tatooings (which were used by the Thracicans and by the ancient inhabitants of Constantinople, and which were forbidden by Moses, *Levit. xix.* 28.) were only displayed by Southern races as a kind of war-paint.

Like the Gauls, who endeavored to make their bright red hair rough and bristly not for ornament, but as a terror to their enemies, these Britons on the day of battle flung off their clothes, and with swords girded to their naked sides, and spear in hand, marched with joyful cries against their enemies.

Also upon certain festivals they, with their wives and children, daubed themselves from head to foot with the blue dye of the woad and danced in circles bowing to the altar.

But the Picts, or painted men, as the Romans named them, colored themselves with the juice of green grass.

Hunting was their favorite exercise and sport, and Britain which was then filled with vast swamps and forests afforded them a variety of game.

The elephant and the rhinoceros, the moose-deer, the tiger and other beasts now only known in Eastern climes, and mammoth creatures that have since disappeared from the face of the earth made the ground tremble beneath their stately tread. The brown bear preyed upon their cattle, and slept in the hollow oaks which they revered. The hyenas yelped by night, and prowled round the fold of the shepherd. The beaver fished in their streams, and built its earthen towns upon their banks. And hundreds of wolves, united by the keen frosts of winter, gathered round the rude habitations of men and howled from fierce hunger, rolling their horrible green eyes and gnashing their white teeth.

Their seas abounded with fish, but since they held water sacred they would not, injure its inhabitants for they believed them to be spirits.

.   .   .   .

I will now consider the primeval state of trade in Britain, now the greatest commercial country in the world.

It was periodically visited by the Phœnicians, a crafty and enterprising nation whose commerce embraced the whole of the known world, from the frozen borders of Scythia to the burning coasts of Africa and Hindostan; whose vessels like the Spanish galleons and our own East Indiamen of old were equipped equally for trade or war; who robbed the weak with their drawn swords, and the strong with their cunning arts; who traded with Arabia for spices and precious stones; with Damascus for the Mesopotamian white wool, and for wine of Aleppo, a beverage so costly that it was drunk by kings alone: with Judœa for fruits of the soil, corn, grape-honey, oil and balm; with Armenia for mules and

chariot-horses, flocks and herds; with the shores of
the Baltic for amber; with Spain for minerals; with
the Euxine for tunny-fish; with India for the cinnamon of Ceylon, for cotton garments and for steel
which sold in Arabia for twice its weight in gold,
and of which the Damascus blades so celebrated in
the middle ages were made.

It was not long before they discovered the lead
and tin mines of Cornwall and the Cassiterides,
which would appear (from several flint-headed tools
called *celts* lately discovered within them) to have
been worked by the Britons themselves.

And as they were wont to exchange the pottery
of Athens for the ivory of Africa, and live Jews for
the gold and jewels of the Greeks, so they bartered
salt, earthenware and brazen trinkets with the Britons
for tin, lead, and the skins of wild beasts.

It was the policy of the Phœnicians (in which they
were afterwards imitated by the Dutch) to preserve
their commercial secrets with the greatest jealousy,
and to resort to extremes in order to protect their
interests. Although they had supplied tin and amber
for several years to the Greeks, Herodotus, who had
visited Tyre, could only obtain very vague accounts
as to the countries from which they had been obtained, and on making inquiries respecting cinnamon
and frankincense, was explicitly informed that the

first was procured by stratagem from the nests of birds built upon inaccessible crags, and the latter from a tree guarded by winged serpents.

There is also the story of the master of a Phœnician trader from Cadiz to the Cassiterides, who finding himself followed by a Roman ship ran his own vessel ashore preferring death to discovery. The Romans were also shipwrecked, and were drowned, but the patriot escaped to tell his tale at Tyre, and to receive from a grateful state the value of his cargo and an additional reward.

In spite of these precautions, either by accident, or by the treachery of some renegado Phœnician, or from the colony of Phocians at Marseilles, the Greeks discovered the secret about three hundred years before the Christian era.

Thus monopoly being ended, the commerce of the Britons was extended and improved, and after the descent of the Romans they exported not only tin and lead, but also gold, silver, iron, corn, cattle, slaves hunting-dogs, pearls, and those wicker baskets which Martial has immortalized in his epigrams.

It also appears that chalk was an article of their trade, by this inscription which was found with many others near Zeland, A. D. 1647.

DEAE NEHALENNIAE
OB MERCES RECTE CONSER
VATAS SECVND SILVANVS
NEGO X TOR CRETARIVS
BRITANNICIANUS
V. S· L· M.

To the Goddess Nehalennia
For his goods well preserved
Secundus Silvanus
A chalk merchant
Of Britain
Willingly performed his merited vow.

Before describing the religion and superstitions of our earliest ancestors, which will bring me to the real purpose of this book, I will add a few remarks upon their manners and peculiarities.

Curiosity, which is certainly the chief characteristic of all barbarous and semi-barbarous nations, was possessed by the Celts in so extraordinary a degree that they would compel travelers to stop, even against their wills, and make them tell some news, and deliver an opinion upon the current events of the day. They would also crowd round the merchants in towns with the same kind of inquiries.

But the great failing of these Celts was their hastiness and ferocity. Not content with pitched battles against their enemies abroad, they were always ready to fight duels with their friends at home. In

fact, the end of a British feast was always the beginning of a fray; two warriors would rise and fight
each other with such *sang-froid* that Athenœus
wrote in astonishment, *Mortem pro joco habent*,
"They turn death into a joke;" and it was from
these spectacles that the Romans conceived and
executed the idea of gladiatorial entertainments.

They feared nothing these brave men.   They
sang as they marched to battle, and perhaps to death.
They shot arrows at the heavens when it thundered;
they laughed as they saw their own hearts' blood
gushing forth.

And yet they were plain and simple in their manners; open and generous, docile and grateful,
strangers to low cunning and deceit, so hospitable
they they hailed the arrival of each fresh guest with
joy and festivities, so warm-hearted that they were
never more pleased than when they could bestow a
kindness.

Their code of morals, like those of civilized nations, had its little contradictions; they account it
disgraceful to steal, but honorable to rob, and though
they observed the strictest chastity, they did not
blush to live promiscuously in communities of
twelve.

This extraordinary custom induced Cæsar to assert
that they enjoyed each other's wives in common;

but in this he is borne out by no other authorities, and, indeed, there are many instances of this kind among barbarous nations, who love, apparently, to hide their real purity with a gross and filthy enamel.

Richard of Circencester (probably alluding to Bath the *aquæ solis* of the ancients) mentions, however, some salt and warm springs used by the ancient Britons, from which were formed hot baths suited to all ages, with distinct places for the two sexes; a refinement which was unknown in Lacedœmon.

And Procopius writes:—

" So highly rated is chastity among these barbarians, that if even the bare mention of marriage occurs without its completion, the maiden seems to lose her fair fame."

Having thus briefly sketched the condition and employments of the early Britons—having proved that our ancestors were brave, and that their daughters were virtuous, I will now show you those wise and potent men of whom these poor barbarians were but the disciples and the slaves.

BOOK THE THIRD.

THE DRUIDS.

I.

ORIGIN.

A LTHOUGH the term *Druid* is local, their religion was of deep root, and a distant origin.
It was of equal antiquity with those of the Persian
Magi, the Chaldees of Assyria, and the Brachmans
of Hindostan.

It resembled them so closely in its sublime precepts, in its consoling promises, as to leave no doubt
that these nations, living so widely apart, were all of
the same stock and the same religion—that of Noah,
and the children of men before the flood.

They worshipped but one God, and erected to him
altars of earth, or unhewn stone, and prayed to him
in the open air; and believed in a heaven, in a hell,
and in the immortality of the soul.

It is strange that these offsprings of the patriarchs
should also be corrupted from the same sources, and
should thus still preserve a resemblance to one another in the minor tenets of their polluted creeds.

Those pupils of the Egyptian priests, the Phœnicians, or Canaanites, who had taught the Israelites to sacrifice human beings, and to pass their children through the fire to Moloch, infused the same blood-thirsty precepts among the Druids. As the Indian wife was burnt upon her husband's pyre, so, on the corpses of the Celtic lords, were consumed their children, their slaves, and their horses.

And, like the other nations of antiquity, as I shall presently prove, the Druids worshipped the heavenly bodies, and also trees, and water, and mountains, and the signs of the serpent, the bull and the cross.

The doctrine of the transmigration of souls which formed a leading theory on the system of the Brachmans, of the Druids, and afterwards of the Pythagoreans was obtained, through the Phœnicians, from Egypt, the fatherland of heathen mythology.

It cannot be denied that they also honored inferior deities, to whom they gave the names of Hu and Ceridwen, Hesus Taranis, Belenus, Ogmius, and the attributes of Osiris and Isis (or Zeus and Venus) Bacchus, Mercury, Apollo, and Hercules.

From the sandy plains of Egypt to the icebergs of Scandinavia, the whole world has rung with the exploits of Hercules, that invincible god, who but appeared in the world to deliver mankind from monsters and from tyrants.

He was really a Phœnician *harokel*, or merchant,

an enterprising mariner, and the discoverer of the tin mines of the Cassiterides. He it was who first sailed through the Straits of Gibraltar, which, to this day, are called *The Pillars of Hercules*: who built the first ship: who discovered the mariner's compass, and the loadstone, or *lapes Heraclius*.

It is gratifying to learn that his twelve labors were, in reality, twelve useful discoveries, and that he had not been deified for killing a wild beast and cleaning out stables.

As the Chaldeans, who were astronomers, made Hercules an astronomer; and as the Greeks and Romans, who were warriors, made him a hero of battles; so the Druids, who were orators, named him *Ogmius*, or the Power of Eloquence, and represented him as an old man followed by a multitude, whom he led by slender and almost invisible golden chains fastened from his lips to their ears.

As far as we can learn, however, the Druids paid honors, rather than adoration to their deities, as the Jews revered their arch-angels, but reserved their worship for Jehovah.

And, like the God of the Jews, of the Chaldees, of the Hindoos, and of the Christians, this Deity of the Druids had three attributes within himself, and each attribute was a god.

Let those learn who cavil at the mysterious doctrine of the Trinity, that it was not invented by the Christians, but only by them restored from times of the holiest antiquity into which it had descended from heaven itself.

Although the Druids performed idolatrous ceremonies to the stars, to the elements, to hills, and to trees, there is a maxim still preserved among the Welsh mountaineers, which shows that in Britain the Supreme Being was never so thoroughly forgotten and degraded as he had been in those lands to which he first gave life.

It is one of those sublime expressions which can be but faintly rendered in a foreign language.

" *Nid dim ond duw: nid duw ond dim.*" "God cannot be matter; what is not matter must be God."

V.

POWER.

THIS priesthood flourished in Gaul and in Britain, and in the islands which encircled them.

In whichever country they may first have struck root we at least know that the British Druids were the most famous, and that it was a custom in the time of Julius Cæsar for the Gallic students to cross the British channel to study in the seminaries of the sister island.

But by that time, Druidism had begun to wane in Gaul, and to be deprived of many of its privileges by the growing intelligence of the secular power.

It is generally acknowledged that there were no Druids in Germany, though Keysler has stoutly contested this belief and has cited an ancient tradition to the effect that they had Druidic colleges in the days of Hermio, a German Prince.

The learned Selden relates that some centuries ago in a monastery upon the borders of Vaitland, in Germany, were found six old statues which being exposed to view, Conradus Celtes, who was present, was of opinion that they were figures of ancient Druids. They were seven feet in height, bare-footed, their heads covered with a Greek hood, a scrip by their sides and a beard descending from their nostrils plaited out in two divisions to the middle; in their hands a book and a Diogenes staff five feet in length; their features stern and morose; their eyes lowered to the ground.

Such evidence is mere food for conjecture. Of the ancient German priests we only know that they resembled the Druids, and the medicine-men of the American aborigines in being doctors as well as priests.

The Druids possessed remarkable powers and immunities. Like the Levites, the Hebrews, and the Egyptian priests they were exempted from taxes and from military service. They also annually elected the magistrates of cities: they educated all children of whatever station, not permitting their parents to receive them till they were fourteen years of age. Thus the Druids were regarded as the real fathers of the people.

The Persian Magi were entrusted with the education of their sovereign; but in Britain the kings were not only brought up by the Druids, but also relieved by them of all but the odium and ceremonies of sovereignty.

These terrible priests formed the councils of the state, and declared peace or war as they pleased. The poor slave whom they seated on a throne, and whom they permitted to wear robes more gorgeous even than their own was surrounded, not by his noblemen, but by Druids. He was a prisoner in his court, and his jailors were inexorable, for they were priests.

There was a **Chief Druid** to advise him, a bard to sing to him, a *sennechai*, or chronicler, to register his action in the Greek character, and a physician to attend to his health, and to cure or kill him as the state required.

All the priests in Britain and all the physicians, all the judges and all the learned men, all the pleaders in courts of law and all the musicians belonged to the order of the Druids. It can easily be conceived then that their power was not only vast but absolute.

It may naturally excite surprise that a nation should remain so barbarous and illiterate as the Britons undoubtedly were, when ruled by an order of men so polished and so learned.

But these wise men of the West were no less learned in human hearts than in the triplet verses, and oral of their fathers. They imbibed with eagerness the heathen rites of the Phœnician Cabiri, and studied to involve their doctrines and their ceremonies in the deepest mystery. They knew that it is almost impossible to bring women and the vulgar herd of mankind to piety and virtue by the unadorned dictates of reason. They knew the admiration which uneducated minds have always for those things which they cannot understand. They knew that to retain their own sway they must preserve these barren minds in their abject ignorance and superstition.

In all things, therefore, they endeavored to draw a line between themselves and the mass. In their habits, in their demeanor, in their very dress.

They wore long robes which descended to the heel, while that of others came only to the knee; their hair was short and their beards long, while the Britons wore but moustaches on their upper lips, and their hair generally long.

Instead of sandals they wore wooden shoes of a pentagonal shape, and carried in their hands a white wand called *slatan drui' eachd*, or magic wand, and certain mystical ornaments around their necks and upon their breasts.

It was seldom that anyone was found hardy enough to rebel against their power. For such was reserved a terrible punishment. It was called *Excommunication*.

Originating among the Hebrews, and descending from the Druids into the Roman Catholic Church, it was one of the most horrible that it is possible to conceive. At the dead of night, the unhappy culprit was seized and dragged before a solemn tribunal, while torches, painted black, gave a ghastly light, and a low hymn, like a solemn murmur, was chanted as he approached.

Clad in a white robe, the Arch-Druid would rise, and before the assembly of brother-Druids and awe-stricken warriors would pronounce a curse, frightful as a death warrant, upon the trembling sinner. Then they would strip his feet, and he must walk with them bare for the remainder of his days; and would clothe him in black and mournful garments, which he must never change.

Then the poor wretch would wander through the woods, feeding on berries and the roots of trees, shunned by all as if he had been tainted by the plague, and looking to death as a salvation from such cruel miseries.

And when he died, none dared to weep for him; they buried him only that they might trample on his grave. Even after death, so sang the sacred bards, his torments were not ended; he was borne to those regions of eternal darkness, frost, and snow, which, infested with lions, wolves, and serpents, formed the Celtic hell, or *Ifurin*.

These Druids were despots; and yet they must

have exercised their power wisely and temperately to have retained so long their dominion over a rude and warlike race.

There can be little doubt that their revenues were considerable, though we have no direct means of ascertaining this as a fact.   However, we know that it was customary for a victorious army to offer up the chief of its spoils to the gods; that those who consulted the oracles did not attend them empty-handed, and that the sale of charms and medicinal herbs was a constant trade among them.

Although all comprehended under the one term DRUID, there were, in reality, three distinct sects comprised within the order.

First, the Druids or Derwydd, properly so called. These were the sublime and intellectual philosophers who directed the machineries of the state and the priesthood, and presided over the dark mysteries of the consecrated groves.

Their name was derived from *derw* (pronounced *derroo*) Celtic for oak, and *ydd*, a common termination of nouns in that language, equivalent to the *or* or *er* in governor, reader, &c., in ours.

The Bards or Bardd from *Bar*, a branch, or, the top.

It was their province to sing the praises of horses in the warrior's feasts, to chant the sacred hymns like the musician's among the Levites, and to register genealogies and historical events.

The Ovades or Ovydd, (derived from *ov*, raw, pure, and *ydd*, above explained) were the noviciates, who, under the supervision of the Druids, studied the properties of nature, and offered up the sacrifices upon the altar.

Thus it appears that Derwydd, Bardd, and Ovydd, were emblematical names of the three orders of Druidism.

The Derwydd was the trunk and support of the whole; the Bardd the ramification from that trunk arranged in beautiful foliage; and the Ovydd was the young shoot, which, growing up, ensured a prospect of permanency to the sacred grove.

The whole body was ruled by an Arch-Druid elected by lot from those senior brethren who were the most learned and the best born.

At Llamdan in Anglesea, there are still vestiges of *Trér Dryw* the Arch-Druid's mansion, *Boadrudau* the abode of the inferior ones, *Bod-owyr* the abode of the ovades, and *Trér-Beirdd* the hamlet of the bards.

Let us now consider these orders under their respective denominations—Derwydd, Bardd, Ovyd; and under their separate vocations, as philosophers musicians, and priests.

VI.

THE DERWYDD, OR PHILOSOPHERS.

DRUIDISM was a religion of philosophy; its high-priests were men of learning and science. Under the head of the Ovydd, I shall describe their initiatory and sacrificial rites, and shall now merely consider their acquirements, as instructors, as mathematicians, as law-givers and as physicians.

Ammianus Marcellinus informs us that the Druids dwelt together in fraternities, and indeed it is scarcely possible that they could have lectured in almost every kind of philosophy and preserved their arcana from the vulgar, unless they had been accustomed to live in some kind of convent or college.

They were too wise, however, to immure themselves wholly in one corner of the land, where they would have exercised no more influence upon the nation than the Heads and Fellows of our present universities. While some lived the lives of hermits in caves and in hollow oaks within the dark recesses of the holy forests; while others lived peaceably in their college-home, teaching the bardic verses to children, to the young nobles, and to the students who came to them from a strange country across the sea, there were others who led an active and turbulent existence at court in the councils of the state and in the halls of nobles.

In Gaul, the chief seminaries of the Druids was in the country of the Carnutes between Chartres and Dreux, to which at one time scholars resorted in such numbers that they were obliged to build other academies in various parts of the land, vestiges of which exist to this day, and of which the ancient College of Guienne is said to be one.

When their power began to totter in their own country, the young Druids resorted to Mona, now Anglesea, in which was the great British university, and in which there is a spot called *Myrfyrion*, the seat of studies.

The Druidic precepts were all in verses, which amounted to 20,000 in number, and which it was forbidden to write. Consequently a long course of preparatory study was required, and some spent so much as twenty years in a state of probation.

These verses were in rhyme, which the Druids invented to assist the memory, and in a triplet form from the veneration which was paid to the number three by all the nations of antiquity.

In this the Jews resembled the Druids, for although they had received the written law of Moses, there was a certain code of precept among them which was taught by mouth alone, and in which those who were the most learned were elevated to the Rabbi.

The mode of teaching by memory was also practised by the Egyptians and by Lycurgus, who esteemed it better to imprint his laws on the minds of the Spartan citizens than to engrave them upon tablets. So, too, were Numa's sacred writing buried with him by his orders, in compliance perhaps with the opinions of his friend Pythagoras who, as well as Socrates, left nothing behind him committed to writing.

It was Socrates, in fact, who compared written doctrines to pictures of animals which resemble life, but which when you question them can give you no reply.

But we who love the past have to lament this system. When Cambyses destroyed the temples of Egypt, when the disciples of Pythagoras died in the Meta-pontine tumults, all their mysteries and all their learning died with them.

So also the secrets of the Magi, the Orpheans and the Cabiri perished with their institutions, and it is owing to this law of the Druids that we have only the meagre evidence of ancient authors and the obscure emblems of the Welsh Bards, and the faint vestiges of their mighty monuments to teach us concerning the powers and direction of their philosophy.

There can be no doubt that they were profoundly learned. For ordinary purposes of writing, and in the keeping of their accounts on the Alexandrian method, they used the ancient Greek character of which Cadmus, a Phœnician, and Timagines, a Druid, were said to have been the inventors and to have imported into Greece.

This is a fac-simile of their alphabet as preserved in the *Thesaurus Muratori*. Vol. IV. 2093.

Both in the universities of the Hebrews, which existed from the earliest times, and in those of the Brachmans it was not permitted to study philosophy and the sciences, except so far as they might assist the student in the perusal and comprehension of the sacred writings. But a more liberal system existed among the Druids, who were skilled in all the arts and in foreign languages.

For instance, there was Abaris, a Druid and a native of the Shetland Isles who traveled into Greece, where he formed a friendship with Pythagoras and where his learning, his politeness, his shrewdness, and expedition in business, and above all, the ease and elegance with which he spoke the Athenian tongue, and which (so said the orator Himerius) would have made one believe that he had been brought up in the academy or the Lycœum, created for him as great a sensation as that which was afterwards made by the admirable Crichton among the learned doctors of Paris.

It can easily be proved that the science of astronomy was not unknown to the Druids. One of their temples in the island of Lewis in the Hebrides, bears evident signs of their skill in the science. Every stone in the temple is placed astronomically. The circle consists of twelve equistant obelisks denoting the twelve signs of the zodiac. The four cardinal points of the compass are marked by lines of obelisks running out from the circle, and at each point subdivided into four more. The range of obelisks from north, and exactly facing the south is double, being two parallel rows each consisting of nineteen stones. A large stone in the centre of the circle, thirteen feet high, and of the perfect shape of a ship's rudder would seem as a symbol of their knowledge of astronomy being made subservient to navigation, and the Celtic word for star, *ruth-iul*, "a-guide-to-direct-the-course," proves such to have been the case.

This is supposed to have been the winged temple which Erastosthenes says that Apollo had among the Hyperboreans—a name which the Greeks applied to all nations dwelling north of the Pillars of Hercules.

But what is still more extraordinary, Hecateus makes mention that the inhabitants of a certain Hyperborian island, little less than Sicily, and over against Celtiberia—a description answering exactly to that of Britain—could bring the moon so near them as to show the mountains and rocks, and other appearances upon its surface.

According to Strabo and Bochart, glass was a discovery of the Phœnicians and a staple commodity of their trade, but we have some ground for believing that our philosophers bestowed rather than borrowed this invention.

Pieces of glass and crystal have been found in the cairns, as if in honor to those who invented it; the process of vitrifying the very walls of their houses, which is still to be seen in the Highlands prove that they possessed the art in the gross; and the Gaelic name for glass is not of foreign but of Celtic extraction, being *glasine* and derived from *glas-theine*, glued or brightened by fire.

We have many wonderful proofs of the skill in mechanics. The *clacha-brath*, or rocking-stones, were spherical stones of an enormous size, and were raised upon other flat stones into which they inserted a small prominence fitting the cavity so exactly, and so concealed by loose stones lying around it, that nobody could discern the artifice.   Thus these globes were balanced so that the slightest touch would make them vibrate, while anything of greater weight pressing against the side of the cavity rendered them immovable.

In Iona, the last asylum of the Caledonian Druids, many of these *clacha-brath* (one of which is mentioned in Ptolemy Hephestion's History, Lib. iii. cap 3.) were to be found at the beginning of this century, and although the superstitious natives defaced them and turned them over into the sea, they considered it necessary to have something of the kind in their stead, and have substituted for them rough stone balls which they call by the same name.

In Stonehenge, too, we find an example of that oriental mechanism which is displayed so stupendously in the pyramids of Egypt.   Here stones of thirty or forty tons that must have been a draught for a herd of oxen, have been carried the distance of sixteen computed miles and raised to a vast height, and placed in their beds with such ease that their very mortises were made to tally.

The temples of Abury in Wiltshire, and of Carnac

in Brittany, though less perfect, are even more prodigious monuments of art.

It is scarcely to be wondered at that the Druids should be acquainted with the properties of gun-powder, since we know that it was used in the mysteries of Isis, in the temple of Delphi, and by the old Chinese philosophers.

Lucan in his description of a grove near Marseilles, writes:—" There is a report that the grove is often shaken and strangely moved, and that dreadful sounds are heard from its caverns; and that it is sometimes in a blaze without being consumed."

In Ossian's poem of *Dargo the son of the Druid of Bel*, similar phenomenon are mentioned, and while the Celtic word lightning is *De'lanach*, " the flash or flame of God," they had another word which ex-presses a flash that is quick and sudden as lightning —*Druilanach*, " the flame of the Druids."

It would have been fortunate for mankind had the monks of the middle ages displayed the wisdom of these ancient priests in concealing from fools and madmen so dangerous an art.

.   .   .   .

All such knowledge was carefully retained within the holy circle of their dark caves and forests and which the initiated were bound by a solemn oath never to reveal.

I will now consider the Druids of active life—the preachers, the law-givers, and the physicians.

On the seventh day, like the first patriarchs, they preached to the warriors and their wives from small round eminences, several of which yet remain in different parts of Britain.

Their doctrines were delivered with a surpassing eloquence and in triplet verses, many specimens which are to be found in the Welsh poetry but of which these two only have been preserved by the classical authors.

The first in Pomponius Mela.

> "Ut forent ad bella meliores,
> Æternas esse animas,
> Vitamque alteram ad manes."

> "To act bravely in war,
>   That souls are immortal,
>   And there is another life after death."

The second in Diogenes Laertius.

> ϝεϛειν Θεους
> ηαι μηδεν ηαηον ὀϛαυ
> ηαι ανὀϛειαυ ασηειυ

> "To worship the Gods,
>   And to do no evil,
>   And to exercise fortitude."

Once every year a public assembly of the nation was held in Mona at the residence of the Arch-Druid, and there silence was no less rigidly imposed than in the councils of the Rabbi and the Brachmans. If any one interrupted the orator, a large piece of his robe was cut off—if after that he offended, he was punished with death. To enforce punctuality, like the Cigonii of Pliny, they had the cruel custom of cutting to pieces the one who came last. Their laws, like their religious precepts, were at first esteemed too sacred to be committed to writing—the first written laws being those of Dyrnwal Moelmud, King of Britain, about 440 B. C. and called the Moel-mutian laws; for these were substituted the Mercian code or the laws of Martia, Queen of England, which was afterwards adopted by King Alfred and trans-lated by him into Saxon.

The Manksmen also ascribe to the Druids those excellent laws by which the Isle of Man has always been governed.

The magistrates of Britain were but tools of the Druids, appointed by them and educated by them also; for it was a law in Britain that no one might hold office who had not been educated by the Druids.

The Druids held annual assizes in different parts of Britain (for instance at the monument called *Long Meg and her Daughters* in Cumberland and at the *Valley of Stones* in Cornwall) as Samuel visited Bethel and Gilgal once a year to dispense justice.

There they heard appeals from the minor courts, and investigated the more intricate cases, which sometimes they were obliged to settle by ordeal. The rocking-stones which I have just described, and the walking barefoot through a fire which they lighted on the summit of some holy hill and called *Samb'in*, or the fire of peace, were their two chief methods of testing the innocence of the criminal, and in which they were imitated by the less ingenious and perhaps less conscientious judges of later days.

For previous to the ordeal which they named *GabhaBheil*, or "the trial of Beil," the Druids used every endeavor to discover the real merits of the case, in order that they might decide upon the verdict of Heaven—that is to say, which side of the stone they should press, or whether they should anoint his feet with that oil which the Hindoo priests use in their religious festivals, and which enables the barefoot to pass over the burning wood unscathed.

We may smile at another profanity of the Druids who constituted themselves judges not only of the body but of the soul.

But as Mohammed inspired his soldiers with sublime courage by promising Paradise to those who found a death-bed upon the corpses of their foes, so the very superstitions, the very frauds of these noble Druids tended to elevate the hearts of men towards their God, and to make them lead virtuous lives that they might merit the sweet fields of *Fla'innis*, the heaven of their tribe.

Never before since the world, has such vast power as the Druids possessed been wielded with such purity, such temperance, such discretion.

When a man died a platter of earth and salt was placed upon his breast, as is still the custom in Wales and in the North of Britain.

The earth an emblem of incorruptibility of the body—the salt an emblem of the incorruptibility of the soul.

A kind of court was then assembled round the corpse, and by the evidence of those with whom he had been best acquainted, it was decided with what funeral rites he should be honored.

If he had distinguished himself as a warrior, or as man of science, it was recorded in the death-song; a *cairn* or pile of sacred stones was raised over him, and his arms and tools or other symbols of his profession were buried with him.

If his life had been honorable, and if he had obeyed the three grand articles of religion, the bard sang his *requiem* on the harp, whose beautiful music alone was a pass-port to heaven.

It is a charming idea, is it not? The soul lingering

for the first strain which might release it from the cold corpse, and mingle with its silent ascent to God.

Read how the heroes of Ossian longed for this funereal hymn without which their souls, pale and sad as those which haunted the banks of the Styx, were doomed to wander through the mists of some dreary fen.

When this hymn had been sung, the friends and relatives of the deceased made great rejoicings, and this it was that originated those sombre merry-makings so peculiar to the Scotch and Irish funerals.

.   .   .   .

In the philosophy of medicine, the Derwydd were no less skilled than in sciences and letters. They knew that by means of this divine art they would possess the hearts as well as the minds of men, and obtain not only the awe of the ignorant but also the love of those whose lives they had preserved.

Their sovereign remedy was the missoldine or mistletoe of the oak which, in Wales, still bears its ancient name of *Oll-iach*, or all-heal, with those of *Pren-awr*, the celestial tree, and *Uchelwydd*, the lofty shrub.

When the winter has come and the giant of the forest is deserted by its leaves and extends its withered arms to the sky, a divine hand sheds upon it

from heaven a mysterious seed, and a delicate green
plant sprouts from the bark, and thus is born while
all around is dying and decayed.

We need not wonder that the mistletoe should be
revered as a heaven-born plant, and as a type of
God's promise and consolation to those who were
fainting on death's threshold in the winter of old
age.

When the new year approached, the Druids beset
themselves to discover this plant upon an oak, on
which tree it grows less frequently than upon the
ash-crab or apple tree. Having succeeded, and as
soon as the moon was six days old, they marched by
night with great solemnity towards the spot, inviting
all to join their procession with these words: *The
New Year is at hand: let us gather the mistletoe.*

First marched the Ovades in their green sacrificial robes leading two milk-white bullocks. Next
came the bards singing the praises of the Mighty
Essence, in raiment blue as the heavens to which
their hymn ascended. Then a herald clothed in
white with two wings drooping down on each side
of his head, and a branch of vervain in his hand
encircled by two serpents. He was followed by
three Derwydd—one of whom carried the sacrificial
bread—another a vase of water—and the third a
white wand. Lastly, the Arch-Druid, distinguished

by the tuft or tassel to his cap, by the bands hanging from his throat, by the sceptre in his hand and by the golden crescent on his breast, surrounded by the whole body of the Derwydd and humbly followed by the noblest warriors of the land.

An altar of rough stones was erected under the oak, and the Arch-Druid, having sacramentally distributed the bread and wine, would climb the tree, cut the mistletoe with a golden knife, wrap it in a pure white cloth, slay and sacrifice the bullocks, and pray to God to remove his curse from barren women, and to permit their medicines to serve as antidotes for poisons and charms from all misfortunes.

They used the mistletoe as an ingredient in almost all their medicines, and a powder was made from the berries for cases of sterility.

It is a strong purgative well suited to the lusty constitutions of the ancient Britons, but, like bleeding, too powerful a remedy for modern ailments.

With all the herbs which they used for medicine, there were certain mummeries to be observed while they were gathered, which however were not without their object—first in enhancing the faith of the vulgar by exciting their superstitions—and also in case of failure that the patient might be reproached for blundering instead of a physician.

The *vervain* was to be gathered at the rise of the

dog-star, neither sun nor moon shining at the time; it was to be dug up with an iron instrument and to be waved aloft in the air, the left hand only being used.

The leaves, stalks and flowers were dried separately in the shade and were used for the bites of serpents, infused in wine.

The *samulos* which grew in damp places was to be gathered by a person fasting—without looking behind him—and with his left hand. It was laid into troughs and cisterns where cattle drank, and when bruised was a cure for various distempers.

The *selago*, a kind of hedge hyssop, was a charm as well as a medicine. He who gathered it was to be clothed in white—to bathe his feet in running water—to offer a sacrifice of bread and wine—and then with his right hand covered by the skirt of his robe, and with a brazen hook to dig it up by the roots and wrap it in a white cloth.

Prominent among the juggleries of the Druids, stands the serpent's egg—the *ovus anguinum* of Pliny—the *glein neidr* of the ancient Britons—the *adderstone* of modern folk-lore.

It was supposed to have been formed by a multitude of serpents close entwined together, and by the frothy saliva that proceeded from their throats. When it was made, it was raised up in the air by their combined hissing, and to render it efficacious it was to be caught in a clean white cloth before it could fall to the ground—for in Druidism that which touched the ground was polluted. He who performed this ingenious task was obliged to mount a swift horse, and to ride away at full speed pursued by the serpents from whom he was not safe till he had crossed a river.

The Druids tested its virtue by encasing it in gold, and throwing it into a river. If it swam against the stream it would render it possessor superior to his adversaries in all disputes, and obtain for him the friendship of great men.

The implicit belief placed in this fable is curiously exemplified by the fact of a Roman Knight of the Vocontii, while pleading his own cause in a law suit was discovered with one of these charms in his breast and was put to death upon the spot.

Their reverence for the serpent's egg has its origin in their mythology. Like the Phœnicians and Egyptians, they represented the creation by the figure of an egg coming out of a serpent's mouth, and it was doubtless the excessive credulity of the barbarians which tempted them to invent the above fable that they might obtain high prices for these amulets, many of which have been discovered in Druidic barrows, and are still to be met with in the

Highlands, where a belief in their power has not yet subsided; for it is no uncommon thing when a distemper rages among men or beasts, for the *Glass-physician* to be sent for from as great a distance as fifty miles.

These eggs are made of some kind of glass or earth glazed over, and are sometimes blue, green, or white, and sometimes variegated with all these colors intermixed.

For mental disorders and some physical complaints they used to prescribe pilgrimages to certain wells, always situated at a distance from the patient, and the waters of which were to be drunk and bathed in. With these ablutions, sacred as those of the Musselmen, were mingled religious ceremonies with a view to remind them of the presence of that God who alone could relieve them from their infirmities. After reaching the wells, they bathed thrice—that mysterious number—and walked three times round the well, *deis'iul*, in the same direction as the course of the sun, also turning and bowing from East to West.

These journeys were generally performed before harvest, at which time the modern Arabs go through a series of severe purgings, and when English laborers, twenty years ago, used systematically to go to the market town to be bled.

The season of the year—the exercise—the mineral
in the water—above all the strong faith of the patients
effected so many real cures that in time it became a
custom (still observed in Scotland with the well of
Strathfillan and in many parts of Ireland) for all who
were afflicted with any disorder to perform an annual
pilgrimage to these holy wells.

Caithbaid, an Irish historian, speaks of the Druid
Trosdan who discovered an antidote for poisoned
arrows, and there are many instances on record of
the medicinal triumphs of the Druids.

They were more anxious to prevent disease than
to cure them, and issued many maxims relating to the
care of the body, as wise as those which appertained
to the soul were divine.

Of these I will give you one which should be
written in letters of Gold.

Bi gu sugach geanmnaidh mocheir' each.

Cheerfulness, temperance and early rising.

VII.

THE BARDD, OR MUSICIANS.

A S there were musicians among the Levites, and priests among the Phœnicians who chanted bare-foot and in white surplices the sacred hymns, so there were bards among the Druids.

Who were divided into three classes.

I. The *Fer-Laoi*, or Hymnists, who sang the essence and immortality of the soul; the works of nature; the course of the celestial bodies; with the order and harmony of the spheres.

II. The *Senachies* who sang the fabulous histories of their ancestors in rude stanzas, and who with letters cut from the bark of trees inscribed passing events and became the historians of their nation.

The *Fer-Dan* who were accustomed to wander through the country, or to be numbered in the retinues of kings and nobles, who not only sang enconiums upon the great warriors of the age, but who wrote satires upon the prevailing vices, worthy of a Juvenal or a Horace.

I can best give the reader some idea of the style and power of their conceptions, by quoting some of their axioms which have descended to us traditionally.

They are in the form of Triads, of which the subjects are, language—fancy and invention—the design of poetry—the nature of just thinking—rules of arrangement—method of description—*e. g.*

The three qualifications of poetry—endowment of genius, judgment from experience, and happiness of mind.

The three foundations of judgment—bold design, frequent practice, and frequent mistakes.

The three foundations of learning—seeing much, studying much, and suffering much.

The three foundations of happiness—a suffering with contentment, a hope that it will come, and a belief that it will be.

The three foundations of thought—perspicuity, amplitude, and preciseness.

The three canons of perspicuity—the word that is necessary, the quantity that is necessary, and the manner that is necessary.

The three canons of amplitude—appropriate thought, variety of thought and requisite thought.

How full of wisdom and experience! what sublime ideas in a few brief words!

These poets were held in high honor by the Britons, for among a barbarous people musicians are angels who bring to them a language from the other world, and who alone can soften their iron hearts and fill their bold blue eyes with gentle tears.

There is an old British law commanding that all should be made freedmen of slaves who were of these three professions. A scholar learned in the languages—a bard—or a smith. When once the smith had entered a smithy, or the scholar had been polled, or the bard had composed a song, they could never more be deprived of their freedom.

Their ordinary dress was brown, but in religious ceremonies they wore ecclesiastical ornaments called *Bardd-gwewll*, which was an azure robe with a cowl to it—a costume afterwards adopted by the lay monks of Bardsey Island (the burial-place of Myrrddin or Merlin) and was by them called *Cyliau Duorn*, or black cowls; it was then borrowed by the Gauls and is still worn by the Capuchin friars.

Blue which is an emblem of the high heavens and the beautiful sea had always been a favorite color with the ancient Britons, and is still used as a toilet paint by the ladies of Egypt and Tartary. Blue rosettes are the insignia of our students in the twin universities, and for the old Welsh proverb. *Y gwer las ni chyll môi liu,* "True blue keeps its hue," one of our proverbial expressions may be traced.

The harp, or lyre, invented by the Celts had four or five strings, or thongs made of an ox's hide, and was usually played upon with a plectrum made of the jaw-bone of a goat. But we have reason to believe that it was the instrument invented by Tubal which formed the model of the Welsh harps.

Although the Greeks (whom the learned Egyptians nicknamed "children," and who were the most vain-glorious people upon the earth) claimed the harp as an invention of their ancient poets, Juvenal in his third satire acknowledges that both the Romans and the Greeks received it from the Hebrews. This queen of instruments is hallowed to our remembrance by many passages in the Bible. It was from the harp that David before Saul drew such enchanting strains that the monarch's heart was melted and the dark frown left his brow. It was on their harps that the poor Jewish captives were desired to play, on their harps which swayed above them on the branches of the willow trees while the waters of Babylon sobbed past beneath their feet.

And it was the harp which St. John beheld in the white hands of the angels as they stood upon the sea of glass mingled with fire, singing the song of Moses, the servant of God, and the song of the lamb.

The trunks of these harps were polished and in
the shape of a heart; they were embraced between
the breast and the arm; their strings were of glossy
hair. In Palestine they were made from the wood
of the Cedars of Lebanon; in Britain of *Pren-masarn*,
or the sycamore.

In their construction, the same mysterious regard
was paid to the number three. Their shape was
triangular; their strings were three in number, and
their turning keys had three arms.

In later times the Irish, who believe that they are
descended from David, obtained an European fame
for their skill in the making of this instrument.
Dante mentions the circumstance, and the harp is
still a mint-mark upon Irish coin.

The Bards from what we can learn of them, neither
debased their art to calumny nor to adulation, but
were in every way as worthy of our admiration as
those profound philosophers to whom alone they
were inferior.

We learn that, (unlike the artists of later times)
they were peculiarly temperate, and that in order to
inure themselves to habits of abstinence they would
have all kinds of delicacies spread out as if for a banquet, and upon which having feasted their eyes for
some time they would order to be removed.

Also that they did their utmost to stay those civil

wars which were the bane of Britain, and that often when two fierce armies had stood fronting each other in array of battle, their swords drawn, their spears pointing to the foe and waiting but for the signal from their chieftains to begin the conflict, the Bards had stepped in between and had touched their harps with such harmony, and so persuaded them with sweet thrilling verses, that suddenly, on either side soldiers had dropped their arms and forgotten the fierce resentment which had been raging in their breasts.

VIII.

THE OVADES, OR NOVICIATES.

IN writing of the Derwydd, or philosophers, I have written also of the high priests, or magicians—for *magnus* is but another name for priest, and in the Chinese and various hieroglyphical languages, the same sign represents a magician and a priest.

I have now to describe the lower order of *sacrificers* who, under the direction of their masters, slew the victims upon the altar, and poured out the sacramental wine.

The Ovades were usually dressed in white, while their sacerdotal robes were of green, an ancient emblem of innocence and youth, still retained in our language, but debased and vulgarized into slang.

They are generally represented with chaplets of oak-leaves on their brows, and their eyes modestly fixed on the ground.

Having been carefully trained in the Druidic seminaries, their memory being stored with the holy triads, and with the outward ceremonies of their religion, they were prepared for initiation into the sublime mysteries of Druidism.

During a period of probation, the Ovade was closely watched; eyes, to him invisible, were ever upon him, noting his actions and his very looks, searching into his heart for its motive, and into his soul for its abilities.

He was then subjected to a trial so painful to the body, so terrible to the mind, that many lost their senses for ever, and others crawled back to the daylight pale and emaciated, as men who had grown old in prison.

These initiations took place in caves, one of which still exists in Denbighshire. We have also some reason to believe that the catacombs of Egypt and those artificial excavations which are to be found in many parts of Persia and Hindostan were constructed for the same purpose.

The Ovade received several wounds from a man who opposed his entrance with a drawn sword. He was then led blind-folded through the winding alleys of the cave which was also a labyrinth. This was intended to represent the toilsome wanderings of the soul in the mazes of ignorance and vice.

Presently the ground would begin to rock beneath his feet; strange sounds disturbed the midnight silence. Thunder crashed upon him like the fall of an avalanche, flashes of green lightning flickered through the cave displaying to his view hideous spectres arrayed against the walls.

Then lighted only by these fearful fires a strange procession marched past him, and a hymn in honor of the Eternal Truth was solemnly chanted by unseen tongues.

Here the profounder mysteries commenced. He was admitted through the North Gate or that of Cancer, where he was forced to pass through a fierce fire. Thence he was hurried to the Southern Gate or that of Capricorn, where he was plunged into a flood, and from which he was only released when life was at its last gasp.

Then he was beaten with rods for two days, and buried up to his neck in snow.

This was the baptism of fire, of water, and of blood.

Now arrived on the verge of death, an icy chill seizes his limbs; a cold dew bathes his brow, his faculties fail him; his eyes close; he is about to faint, to expire, when a strain of music, sweet as the distant murmur of the holy brooks, consoling as an angel's voice, bids him to rise and to live for the honor of his God.

Two doors with a sound like the fluttering of wings are thrown open before him. A divine light bursts upon him, he sees plains shining with flowers open around him.

Then a golden serpent is placed in his bosom as a sign of his regeneration, and he is adorned with a mystic zone upon which are engraved twelve mysterious signs; a tiara is placed upon his head; his form naked and shivering is clothed in a purple tunic studded with innumerable stars; a crozier is placed in his hand. He is a king; for he is initiated; for he is a Druid.

IX.

RITES AND CEREMONIES.

A RELATION of the duties of the Ovades as sacrificers will naturally lead us into a description of the ceremonies of the priesthood, of their altars, their temples and their objects of worship or veneration.

The *clachan*, or stone temples of the Druids were round like those of the Chinese, the primitive Greeks, the Jews, and their copyists the Templars. This shape was adopted because it was typical of eternity, and also of the solar light—the word *circus* being derived from the Phœnician *cir* or *cur*, the Sun.

Like those of the Thracians they were open at the roof, for the Druids deemed it impious to attempt to enclose within a house that God, whose shrine was the universe.

There were two celebrated temples of the Druids, Abury in Wiltshire, and Carnac in Brittany, which were built in the form of a serpent.

There is scarcely a spot in the world in which the

serpent has not received the prayers and praises of men. At first an emblem of the sun's light and power, it is worshipped in lands where the sun is not recognized as a Deity, for instance on the coasts of Guinea where the negroes curse him every morning as he rises, because he scorches them at noon.

The winged serpent was a symbol of the Gods of Egypt, Phœnicia, China, Persia, and Hindostan. The Tartar princes still carry the image of a serpent upon a spear as their military standard. Almost all the Runic inscriptions found upon tombs are engraved upon the sculptured forms of serpents. In the temple of the Bona Dea, serpents were tamed and consecrated. In the mysteries of Bacchus, women used to carry serpents in their hands and twined around their brows, and with horrible screams cry, *Eva! Eva!* In the great temple of Mexico, the captives taken in war and sacrificed to the sun, had wooden collars in the shape of a serpent put round their necks. And water-snakes are to this day held sacred by the natives of the Friendly Isles.

It was not only worshipped as a symbol of light, of wisdom and of health, personified under the name of God, but also as an organ of divination. Serpents formed the instruments of the Egyptian enchanters, the *fetich* of the Hottentots, and the girdles of the medicine-men of the North American Indians. The

Norwegians, too, of the present day, when hunting will often load their guns with serpents to make them fortunate.

The serpent must have obtained this world-wide worship from its beauty, and its wisdom. Subtle in heart beyond all the beasts of the field; rapid and mysterious in its wary footless movements, to which the ancients were wont to resemble the aerial progress of the Gods; above all its eyes so bright, so lovely, so weird in their powers of facinations, no wonder that it should excite the awe and admiration of superstitious barbarians.

And they believed it immortal, for every year they saw it cast its skin, wrinkled and withered with age, and when they tried to kill it they found that it retained life with miraculous pertinacity.

Finally it was the brazen serpent elevated upon a cross that Moses erected in the wilderness, and upon which all who gazes were saved from death; and it was this serpent which Jewish and Christian writers have agreed in asserting to be a type of the Messiah.

The *cromleachs* were the altars of the Druids, and were so called from a Hebrew word signifying, "to bow," and from the bowing of the worshippers who believed them to be guarded by spirits.

They were constructed of a large flat stone placed

upon two rough pillars. These stones were always unhewn, for by the Druidic law it was ordained that no axe should touch the sacred stones, a precept which very strangely coincides with the Mosaic law. " *Thou shalt not build an altar of hewn stones.*" Exod. xx, 25.

These *cromleachs* were also sepulchres, as is testified by the number of urns and human bones that have been discovered beneath some few of them. It is probable that their *clachan* were used for the same purpose, as the Egyptian mummies were interred in the catacombs of the pyramids, and as we bury bodies in the vaults of our churches.

We generally find them situated on hills or mountains, which prove that the Druids entertained the same reverence for high places as the nations of the East, and even the Scandinavians, for we read in the *Erybygga-Saga* that when Thoralf established his colony in the promontory of Thorsness in Iceland he erected an eminence called *Helgafels*, the Holy Mount, upon which none might look till they had made their ablutions under pain of death.

And sometimes by the side of a lake or running stream, for water was held holy by the Druids, and they were even wont to propitiate its deities, by offering it presents.

There was a Druidic temple at Toulouse, on the

borders of a lake into which the Druids threw large quantities of gold, and in which Capion, a Roman knight, and his followers miserably perished in an attempt to recover it. So, *Aurum Tolosanum*, "Gold from Toulouse," became a bye-word among the Romans to express any accident or misfortune.

In the islands surrounding Britain and Gaul, especially in the Channel Islands where they are called *Pouquelays*, these altars are very common. Islands were held sacred for some reason by the ancients.

They were often erected within the recesses of the sacred grove beneath the shadow of an oak.

This, the fairest and strongest of trees has been revered as a symbol of God by almost all the nations of heathendom, and by the Jewish Patriarchs.

It was underneath the oaks of Mamre that Abraham dwelt a long time, and where he erected an altar to God, and where he received the three angels.

It was underneath an oak that Jacob hid the idols of his children, for oaks were held sacred and inviolable. (Judges II. 5. 6.)

From the Scriptures, too, we learn that it was worshipped by the Pagans who corrupted the Hebrews (Hosea. IV. v. 13. Ezekiah VI. 13. Isaiah I. v. 29.)

Homer mentions people entering into compacts

under oaks as places of security. The Grecians had their vocal oaks at Dodona. The Arcadians believed that stirring the waters of a fountain with an oaken bough would bring rain. The Sclavonians worshipped oaks which they enclosed in a consecrated court.

The Romans consecrated the oak to Jupiter their Supreme God, as they consecrated the myrtle to Venus, the laurel to Apollo, the pine to Cybele, the poplar to Hercules, wheat-ears to Ceres, the olive to Minerva, fruits to Pomona, rose-trees to the river nymphs, and hay to poor Vertumnus whose power and merits could obtain him nothing better.

The Hindoos who had no oaks revered the Banian tree.

When an oak died, the Druids stripped off its bark, &c., shaped it reverently into the form of a pillar, a pyramid, or a cross, and still continued to worship it as an emblem of their God.

Besides the *clanchan* and *cromleach* there are many stone monuments remaining in various parts of Gaul and Britain, which bear the Druid stamp in their rudeness and simplicity.

These were sometimes trophies of victory, sometimes memorials of gratitude, sometimes images of God.

When erected they were anointed with rose-oil, as

Jacob anointed the first stone monument on record —that which he raised at Bethel in memory of his dream.

The custom of raising plain stone pillars for idolatrous purposes was afterwards adopted by the Pagans and forbidden by the Mosaic law (Lev. XXVI. 1.)

Mercury, Apollo, Neptune and Hercules were worshipped under the form of a square stone. A large black stone was the emblem of Buddha among the Hindoos, and of Manah Theus-Ceres in Arabia. The Paphians worshipped their Venus under the form of a white pyramid, the Thebans their Bacchus under that of a pillar, the Scandinavians their Odin under that of a cube, the Siamese their Sommonacodum under that of a black pyramid.

And in the temple of the Sun at Cuzco, in Peru, was a stone column in the shape of a cone, which was worshipped as an emblem of the Deity.

Every one has heard of the Stone of Memnon in Egypt, which was said to speak at sun-rise, and the remains of which are covered with inscriptions by Greek and Latin travelers bearing testimony to the fact.

There is a story in Giraldus Cambrensis which proves that the Druids had the same superstition. In his time, a large flat stone ten feet long, six feet wide, and one foot thick served as a bridge over the river Alun at St. David's, in Pembrokeshire. It was called in British *Lech Larar* "the speaking stone," and it was a tradition that if a dead body was carried over the stone it would speak, and that with the struggle of the voice it would crack in the middle, and that then the chink would close.

Keysler informs us that the Northern nations believed their stone deities to be inhabited by fairies or demons, and adduces an instance from the *Holmveria Saga* of Norway.

"Indridus going out of his house lay in wait for his enemy Thorstenus, who was wont to go to the temple of his God at such a particular time. Thorstenus came and, entering the temple before sun-rise, prostrated himself before the stone-deity and offered his devotion. Indridus standing by heard the stone speak, and pronounce Thorstenus' doom in these words:

> Tu huc
> Ultima vice
> Morti vicinis pedibus
> Terram calcasti;
> Certè enim antequam
> Sol splendeat,
> Animosus Indridus
> Odium tibi rependet.

> Heedless of thy approaching fate
> Thou treadst this holy ground;

Last step of life ! thy guilty breast
Ere Phœbus gilds the ruddy East,
    Must expiate
    Thy murderous hate
    Deep pierc'd with crimson wound.

To fire, also, as an emblem of the sun, the Druids paid peculiar reverence.

Indeed fire would appear to have been the chosen element of God.   In the form of a flaming bush He appeared to Moses.   On Mount Sinai His presence was denoted by torrents of flame, and in the form of fire he preceded the little band of Israelites by night, through the dreary wilderness, which is perhaps the origin of the custom of the Arabians who always carry fire in front of their caravans.

All the great nations had their holy fires which were never suffered to die.   In the temple of the Gaditanian Hercules at Tyre, in the Temple of Vesta at Rome, among the Brachmans, the Jews, and the Persians were these immortal fires which might not be desecrated by the breath of men, and which might be fed with peeled wood alone.   So also the American savages when they have gained a victory, would light fires and dance round them.

The Druids thus conducted their worship of the holy element.   Having stripped the bark off dry wood they poured oil of roses upon it, and lighted it by rubbing sticks together, which is said to have been an invention of the Phœnicians.

To this they prayed at certain times, and whoever dared to blow the fire with his mouth, or to throw dirt or dead beasts into it they punished with death.

They had circular temples consecrated to their never-dying fires; into these the priests entered every day, and reverently fed the fire and prayed to it for a whole hour, holding branches of vervain in their hands and crowned with tiaras which hung down in flaps on each side of their faces covering their cheeks and lips.

They also kindled the Beltein, or fire of the rock on May-eve to welcome the sun after his travels behind the clouds and tempests of the dark months. On that night all other fires were extinguished, and all repaired to the holy mount to pay their annual tribute to the Druids.

Then were held solemn rites, and men and beasts, and even goblets of wine were passed through the purifying flames. After which the fires were all relighted, (each from the sacred fire) and general festivity prevailed.

In Cornwall there are *Karn-Gollowa*, the Cairn of Lights, and *Karn-Leskyz*, the Cairn of Burnings which names proves that the fiendish rites of Moloch and Baal were really observed with all their impious cruelty in the island of Britain.

From these same blood-thirsty Phœnicians who

had taught the Israelites to sin, the Druids learnt to pollute their altars with human blood, and to assert that nothing was so pleasing to God as the murder of a man.

In the golden age, men's hearts softened and elevated by gratitude towards their Maker offered him the choicest herbs and the sweetest flowers of the soil.

But in the age of iron, when men had learnt to tremble at their own thoughts, to know that they were thieves, and liars, and murderers, they felt that there was need of expiation.

To appease the God whom they still believed to be merciful, they offered Him *Blood*.

They offered Him the blood of animals.

And then they offered Him the most innocent and beautiful of His creations—beautiful virgins and chaste youths—their eldest sons, their youngest daughters.

Do you disbelieve me? read as I have read all the great writers of the past, and then you will shudder as I have shuddered at such terrible wickedness in man.

Read Manetho, Sanchionatho, Herodotus, Pausanias, Josephus, Philo the Jew, Diodorus of Sicily, Strabo, Cicero, Cæsar, Macrobius, Pliny, Titus Livius, Lucan, and most of the Greek and Latin poets.

Read the books of Leviticus, Deuteronomy, the Judges, Kings, the 105th Psalm, the Prophesies of Isaiah, Jeremiah, Ezekiel, and many of the old fathers, and there you will find that the Egyptians, the Israelites, the Arabs, the Cathaginians, the Athenians, Spartans and Ionians, the Romans, the Scythians, the Albanians, the Germans, Iberians and Gauls had adopted this cruel custom, which like the practice of magic had risen in Phœnicia, and had spread like a plague over the whole world.

The Egyptians sacrificed every year a young and beautiful virgin, whom arrayed in rich robes, they flung into the Nile. They also offered up men with red hair at the shrine of Osiris.

The Spartans whipped boys to death in sight of their parents before starting upon an expedition. The natives of the Tauric Chersonesus hospitably sacrificed to Diana all the strangers whom chance threw upon their coast. The Cimbri ripped their victims open, and divined from their smoking entrails. The Norwegians used to beat their brains out with an axe, the Icelanders by dashing them against a stone. The Scythians cut off the shoulder and arm, and flinging them in the air drew omens from the manner in which they fell upon the pile. The Romans and Persians buried them alive.

This mania for blood was universal. Even The-

mistocles, the deliverer of Greece, had once sacrificed three youths.

The ancient Peruvians, when one of their nation
was dangerously ill, sacrificed his eldest son or
youngest daughter to the solar deity, entreating him
to spare the father's life.   And periodically at their
religious festivals they murdered children and virgins, drowning them and then sacrificing them.

And the ancient Mexicans forced their victims to
lie down upon a pyramidical stone, and tearing out
their hearts, lifted them smoking towards the sun.

I might continue this long and disgusting catalogue
of religious crimes, but let us return to the Druids,
who at least only sacrificed human beings in some
great and peculiar crisis.

The word sacrifice means *an offering of the cake*,
and there can be no doubt that those thin broad
cakes of the ancient Britons, which, with a libation
of flour, milk, eggs, and herbs, or milk, dew and
acorns are still superstitiously offered in the north of
Britain, formed the usual sacrifice.

They also offered the boar, and it is not improbable that the hare, hen and goose which they were
forbidden to eat, but which Cæsar informs us that
they reared *causa voluptatis*, were used for sacrificial
purposes.

The human victims were selected from criminals

or prisoners of war. In lack of these they were chosen by lot, and it sometimes happened that Curtius-like they offered themselves up for their country.

Such a one was led into a sacred forest watered by running streams. In the centre, a circular space surrounded by grey and gigantic stones. Then the birds ceased to sing, the wind was hushed; and the trees around extended their spectral arms which were soon to be sprinkled with human blood.

Then the victim would sing the Song of Death.

The Druid would approach, arrayed in his judicial robes. He was dressed in white; the serpent's egg encased in gold was on his bosom; round his neck was the collar of judgment which would strangle him who delivered an unjust sentence; on his finger was the ring of divination; in his hand was a glittering blade.

They would crown the victim with oak leaves in sombre mockery. They would scatter branches of the oak upon the altar

The voices of the blue-robed Bards would chant a solemn dirge, their harps would tone forth sinister notes.

Pale and stern the Druid would approach, his knife uplifted in the air.

He would stab him in the back. With mournful

music on his lips he would fall weltering in blood, and in the throes of death.

The diviners would draw round, and would calmly augur from his struggles.

After which, fresh oak-leaves would be cast upon the blood-polluted altar, and a death feast would be held near the corpse of the sacrificed.

X.

PRIESTESSES.

THE Druids had many rites of divination—from the entrails of their victims—from the flight of birds—from the waves of the sea—from the bubbling of wells—and from the neighing of white horses.

By the number of criminals causes in the year they formed an estimate of the scarcity or plenty of the year to come.

They also used divining rods, which they cut in the shape of twigs from an apple tree which bore fruit, and having distinguished them from each other by certain marks, threw them promiscuously upon a white garment. Then the Diviner would take up each billet or stick three times, and draw an interpretation from the marks before imprinted on them.

The ordering of these divinations were usually placed in the hands of women who formed an order of Sibylls among these ancient prophets.

It has been the belief of every age that women are more frequently blessed with the gifts of inspiration, and that the mists of the future hang less darkly before their eyes than before those of men.

And thus it was that women were admitted to those holy privileges which none others could obtain except with the learning and struggles of a lifetime, thus it was that even the commonest women was admitted to that shrine from which the boldest warriors were excluded.

There is, however, a tradition that at one period both in Gaul and Britain, the women were supreme, that they ruled the councils of state, that they led the armies of war. That the Druids by degrees supplanted them, and obtained the power for themselves. But to propitiate these women who had the blood of Albina in their veins, they admitted them into their order, and gave them the title of Druidesses.

They were eventually formed into three classes.

I. Those who performed the servile offices about the temple, and the persons of the Druids, and who were not separated from their families.

II. Those who assisted the Druids in their religious services, and who, though separated from their husbands, were permitted to visit them occasionally.

III. A mysterious sisterhood who dwelt in strict chastity and seclusion, and who formed the oracles of Britain.

Such is the origin of Christian mummeries. In all important events the Britons repaired to their dwelling. Not even a marriage was consummated among them without consulting the Druidess, and her *purin*, the seic seona of the Irish, viz., five stones thrown up and caught on the back of the hand, and from which she divined.

There are several instances recorded in classical history of predictions from these priestesses which came true.

Alexander Severus had just set out upon an expedition when he was met by a Druidess, "Go on, my Lord," she said aloud to him as he passed, "but beware of your soldiers."

He was assassinated by his soldiers in that same campaign.

My next example is still more peculiar. When Dioclesian was a private soldier he had a Druidess for hostess, who found him every day reckoning up his accounts with a military exactitude to which the army in those days was a stranger.

"You are niggardly," she said.

"Yes," he answered, "but when I become an Emperor I will be generous."

"You have said no jest," replied the priestess, for you will be Emperor when you have killed a wild boar—*cum aprum occideris.*"

In our language this prophecy loses its point, for there is a play upon the Latin word which cannot be translated. *Aper* means both the name of a man and a wild beast, and thus the prediction was wrapped in that wise ambiguity which has been the characteristic of all human prophecy.

Dioclesian, whose ambition gave him faith, was much perplexed with the double meaning of the word, but hunted assiduously till he had killed so many wild boars, that he began to fear he had taken the word in its wrong acceptation.

So he slew Aper, his stepfather, the assassin of Numerianus, and shortly afterwards sat upon the imperial throne.

In marble, as well as in ink, there are memorials of the sect of Druidesses. The following inscription was discovered at Metz in Normandy:

SILVANO
SACR
ET NYMPHIS LOCI
APETE DRUIS
ANTISTITA
SOMNO MONITA.

Of Druidic oracles we know only of one at Kildare in Ireland; of one at Toulouse which ceased when Christianity was introduced there by St. Saturnins;

of one at Polignac dedicated to Apollo, or Belenus, or Baal; and most celebrated of all that in the island of Sena (now Sain) at the mouth of the River Loire.

This island was inhabited by seven young women who were beautiful as angels, and furious as demons.

They were married but their husbands might never visit them. The foot of man was not permitted to set foot upon their isle.

When the mantle of night had began to descend upon the earth, seven dusky forms might be seen gliding to the shore, and springing into their wicker boats, which were covered with the skins of beasts, would row across to the main-land, and fondle with their husbands, and smile upon them as if with the sweet innocence of youth.

But when the streaks of light began to glimmer in the East, like restless spirits summoned back to their daylight prison, strange fires would gleam from their eyes, and they would tear themselves from their husband's arms.

To them came the sailors who fished and traded on the seas, and entreated them for fair winds. But as they came and as they spoke, they shuddered at the sight of these women whose faces were distorted by inspiration, whose voices seemed to be full of blood.

When Christianity began to prevail in the north, it was believed that these women, by culling certain herbs at various periods of the moon, transformed themselves into winged and raging beasts, and attacking such as were baptized and regenerated by the blood of Jesus Christ, killed them without the visible force of arms, opened their bodies, tore out their hearts and devoured them; then substituting wood or straw for the heart, made the bodies live on as before and returned through the clouds to their island-home.

It is certain that they devoted themselves chiefly to the service of the Moon, who was said to exercise a peculiar influence over storms and diseases—the first of which they pretended to predict, the latter to cure.

They worshipped her under the name of Kêd or Ceridwen, the northern name for the Egyptian Isis.

They consecrated a herb to her, called *Belinuncia*, in the poisonous sap of which they dipped their arrows to render them as deadly as those malignant rays of the moon, which can shed both death and madness upon men.

It was one of their rites to procure a virgin and to strip her naked, as an emblem of the moon in an unclouded sky. They they sought for the wondrous *selago* or golden herb. She who pressed it with her foot slept, and heard the language of animals. If she touched it with iron, the sky grew dark and a misfortune fell upon a world.   When they had found it, the virgin traced a circle round it, and covering her hand in a white linen cloth which had never been before used, rooted it out with a point of her little finger—a symbol of the crescent moon.   Then they washed it in a running spring, and having gathered green branches plunged into a river and splashed the virgin, who was thus supposed to resemble the moon clouded with vapors.   When they retired, the virgin walked backwards that the moon might not return upon its path in the plain of the heavens.

They had another rite which procured them a name as infamous and as terrible as that of the Sirens of the South, who were really Canaanite priestesses that lured men to their island with melodious strains, and destroyed them as a sacrifice to their Gods.

They had a covered temple in imitation probably of the two magnificent buildings which the Greek colonists had erected at Massilia.   This it was their custom annually to unroof, and to renew the covering before the sun set by their united labors.

And if any woman dropt or lost the burden that she was carrying, she was immediately torn to pieces by these savage creatures, who daubed their faces and their white bosoms with their victim's blood, and carried her limbs round the temple with wild and exulting yells.

It was this custom which founded the story told at Athens and at Rome, that in an island of the Northern seas there were virgins who devoted themselves to the service of Bacchus, and who celebrated orgies similar to those of Samothrace.

For in those plays, performed in honor of Dionusus, there was always a representation of a man torn limb from limb. And in the Island of Chios, as in Sena, this drama was enacted to the life.

BOOK THE FOURTH.

THE DESTRUCTION OF THE DRUIDS.

I.

THE DESTRUCTION OF THE DRUIDS.

ON the South coast of Britain the people were thronging by hundreds to the sea-shore. It was to see a vessel which was sailing past, and which had come from some strange country across the seas.

Its prow was adorned with a swan's head and neck made of bronze. Below the prow and projecting a little above the keel was a brazen beak, which was called the *rostrum* and which had been invented by the Tyrrhenian Pisœus for breaking the sides of the enemy's ships.

The stern was elevated and adorned with the figure of a God. There seated, they could distinguish the prominent figure of a man who paddled a huge broad-bladed oar backwards and forwards in the water, and with which he appeared to guide the vessel.

There were two masts made of fire-wood from the forests of Scandinavia, and a triangular sail suspended from each, inflated by the wind.

The sides of this vessel presented an extraordinary sight. Three banks of rowers, raised above each other, were plying their oars which swung in leather thongs, and which surrounded the ship with creamy foam, and which dashed the transparent spray high in the air.

The Britons perched upon the rocks, or in their little wicker boats, continued to watch this ship till it had disappeared, and then returned to their homes to relate this incident to their wives with Celtic garrulity.

It remained to them an enigma, till they received intelligence from the merchants of the main that the ship was a Roman trireme, or war galley; that its commander was Caius Volusenus, and that he had been sent by Julius Cæsar the Divine, to explore the coasts of that country upon which he meditated an invasion.

In fact, it was this great general who, aspiring to outvie the conquests of Pompey, had determined to subdue this island of Britain, which was then only known to the world by some vague and exaggerated reports of the ferocity of its inhabitants, the perils of its seas, the darkness of its sky, and the marvelous beauty of its pearls.

However, the remoteness of the country with the difficulty and danger of the enterprise were those

obstacles which form the stepping-stones to great-
ness; while the precious stones and metals with
which it was said to abound, served to excite the
cupidity of his soldiers whose souls were less open
to those glorious passions which elevated that of
their commander.

The brigands and pirates (that is to say the in-
vaders) of those days even, considered it necessary
to invent a paltry excuse for some act of lawless
oppression; and Cæsar before he attacked the freedom and properties of a nation, affirmed that it was
in revenge for the assistance which a small tribe of
Britons had rendered to his enemies the Gauls.

The Britons terrified by this report, sent ambass—
adors to Rome. Cæsar received them kindly, and
sent Commius, a Roman to whom he had given land
in Gaul, as his ambassador in return.

The Britains violated the law of nations and put
Commius in prison. Cæsar invaded Britain.

Then the groves of the Druids resounded with
the cries of victims, and blood flowed from the knife
of the sacrificer. Then the huge image of a bull
made of wicker-work was erected, and filled with
animals and men, was set on fire, while the drums
and cymbals of the priests drowned those piteous
cries which strange to say was thought ill-omened
to hear.

Then the Bards who before had sung the blessings of peace, and who had parted armies in their fierce strife, sang the war-hymns of their ancestors, and fired every heart with fortitude and emulation.

On the 26th of August, in the year 55 B. C., at about ten o'clock in the forenoon, Cæsar reached the British coasts, where he found the hills covered with armed men.

He sailed along the coast till he came to that low sandy plain on which the town of Deal now stands. It was there that he intended to land, and there that the Britons, perceiving the prows of his vessels turned towards the shore, crowded with horse, foot and chariots to repel him.

The water was too shallow to admit of the galleys approaching close to land. The Romans had therefore to wade through the sea under a cloud of arrows, and fighting with waves as well as with men. Thus they were thrown into disorder, and the waters were reddened with their blood. But Cæsar had commanded the rowing-boats to approach, in which were erected slings with divers instruments of war, and which darted over the water like sharks springing to their prey.

The Britons had begun to yield, but were rallying their courage as they saw that the Romans were fearing those waves which bore past on their dark bosoms the corpses of their comrades. When the standard-bearer of the tenth legion invoked the gods and cried:—" Follow me, if you do not wish me to lose my standard among the foe; but if I lose my life, I shall have done my duty to Rome, and to my general."

The brave man sprang into the sea, with the brazen eagle held aloft, and his bright sword flashing in his hand. The whole legion followed him, and after a long contest obtained a victory which had the Romans possessed cavalry to pursue their routed enemy, would have been as sanguinary as it was glorious and decisive.

From that epoch indeed, Britain may be considered as a Roman state, and its after history as merely the history of its insurrections.

Under Julius Cæsar, the rebellion of Cassebilanus compelled him to make a second expedition against Britain.

Augustus threatened to invade their island if the Britons continued to refuse to pay taxes. Intimidated by his menaces, they sent ambassadors to Rome who implored the pardon of the Emperor, and brought him large gifts, and swore fealty to him in the temple of Mars.

The Britons broke their oath under the reign of Caligula, who made grand preparations for an invasion of the island, but who preferred leading his army against the ocean which he had conquered in this manner.

Having drawn up all his men in battle array upon the seashore, he caused the *balistas*, or slings, and other instruments of war to be ranged before them; he then sailed in a war-galley some little distance into the sea, returned, ordered his trumpeters to sound the charge, and the soldiers to fill their helmets with the shells from the beach, which he stored as the trophies of a conquered enemy in the Capitol. Having commended the courage of his soldiers and rewarded them profusely, he erected a tower upon the spot as if to prevent the nation from forgetting that Cæsar was a madman.

This display of imbecility naturally strengthened the Britons in their resolution to pay no taxes, and to re-assert their freedom.

When Claudius Cæsar came to the throne, he determined (partly on the advice of Bericus, a British outlaw) to invade this rebellious state.

Aulus Plautius was placed at the head of a large army, and after several fierce engagements returned to Rome where he was rewarded with an ovation.

Ostorius was sent to Britain in the same reign to quell an insurrection, and also returned successful, bringing with him Caractacus, its leader, as prisoner.

In the reign of the blood-thirsty Nero, Suetonius was appointed Governor of Britain. For two whole years he made war upon the refractory Britons with great success, subduing fresh tribes and establishing garrisons.

But he had long perceived that there was an influence working against him, which was all the more powerful because it was concealed. It was that of the Druids, who still possessed an extraordinary sway over the minds of British warriors, and who animated them with promises of paradise to the defence of their country and their homes.

He discovered that the chief stronghold of the craft was the island of Mona, now Anglesea. It was to Mona that the British chieftains resorted as an oracle, to learn their destinies and to receive the encouragements of those whom they revered. It was to Mona that the wounded were borne, and were placed under the gentle care of those physicians who knew the secret properties of all herbs and flowers. It was to Mona that the Derwydd, weary with warfare had withdrawn, and for which they had deserted their magnificent seat at Abury, and their circular temple in Salisbury plain.

This island is reported to have been one of the fortunate islands sung of by the Grecian poets, as the Elysian fields. It was watered by clear streams it was clothed with fair meadows like a soft green mantle; it was full of oaken groves sacred to the Gods, from which it was called *Ynys Dewyll* the dark and shadowy island.

It was in the year A. D. 61, that Suetonius resolved to invade this delicious retreat, and to carry the sword into the palace of the Arch-Druid, into the seminary of the Bardic Muse.

He forded the narrow channel which divides the isle from the main-land with his cavalry, while his infantry crossed over in flat-bottomed boats, called *scaphæ*, and by which we learn that they landed near Llamdan where there is a place called *Pant yr yscraphie* to this day.

As the Romans landed, they were petrified by the horrible sight which awaited them.

It was night, and the British army dusky and grim, stood arrayed against them. Women clad in dark and mournful garments, and carrying torches in their hands like the furies of hell, were running up and down the ranks uttering loud wailing cries, while the Druids kneeling before them with hands raised to heaven, made the air resound with frightful imprecations.

At some distance behind them, in the obscurity of a neighboring grove, twinkled innumerable fires.

In these the Roman prisoners were to be burnt alive.

At first, horror-struck, they remained motionless: it was only when their generals exhorted them not to fear a crowd of women and priests, and when a flight of arrows from the Britons assured them that they had really flesh and blood foes to contend with, that they could be brought to advance to the charge with their usual valor and precision.

That night the Druids were burnt in the flames which they themselves had lighted.

But there were many who escaped into the recesses of the sacred groves, or by boat to the neighboring isles. These only waited for an opportunity to excite the Britons to fresh struggles for their freedom, and such an opportunity was soon afforded.

Prasutagus, King of the Iceni, having died, left the half of his property to Cæsar and half to his daughters. This which had been done to obtain the favor of the Romans had an opposite effect. His kingdom and palace were plundered and destroyed, his daughters ravished, his queen beaten like a slave.

The Britons driven to despair by these outrages took arms under Boadicea, the widow of Prasutagus.

Then the image of victory which the Romans had erected, fell down without any apparent cause and backwards as if it would give place to its enemies.

And certain women, distempered with fury, went singing by way of prophecy that destruction was at hand. And strange sounds were heard in the council house of the Romans, and their theatre echoed with hideous howlings, and a bleeding sword was seen in the sky, and a spectre in the arm of the sea, and the ocean was reddened as if with blood, and the shape of men's bodies were left in the sand at the ebb of the tide.

The Britons won several battles, and cruelly massacred all the Romans that they took captive without distinction either of age or sex.

It was already sung by the Bards who accompanied the army with their three-stringed harps that Britain was free.

But Suetonius with his formidable fourteenth legion was as yet unconquered.

With ten thousand men he occupied a strong possession in a pass at the head of an open plain, with a thick wood behind for purposes of retreat and ambush.

Here were drawn up the Roman cavalry, armed after the Greek fashion with spears and bucklers, and the infantry in due order of battle—the *velites* with javelin and target—the *hastati* with their shields and Spanish swords, and coats of mail—and the *triarii* with their pikes.

The British army numbered 230,000 men, which was divided into their infantry, their cavalry, and their war-chariots. The infantry also was divided into three nations, which were subdivided into family tribes resembling the Highland clans.

Those of the South were habited like the Belgic Gauls in woolen tunics thickly woven with coarse harsh wool; their legs and thighs covered with close garments, called *Brachæ*. They wore also helmets of brass, adorned with figures of birds or beasts rudely carved; iron breastplates, protruding with hooks; a long sword hanging obliquely across their thighs; a shield ornamented with figures; and a huge dart whose shaft was of iron, a cubit in length and as broad as two hands put together.

The inland nations were clothed in the skins of beasts and armed with spears and bucklers.

The Caledonians went naked, armed only with long broad pointless swords, and short spears with round balls of brass at the end, with which they used to make a noise before battle to frighten the horses of the enemy.

These Northern nations were of all the most resolute and troublesome enemies of Rome; for they could sleep on bogs covered with water, and live upon the barks and roots of trees, and possessed a peculiar kind of meat, a morsel of which no larger

than a bean could protect them for days from hunger
and thirst.

The cavalry were mounted upon small but hardy
and mettlesome horses, which they managed with
great dexterity.   Their arms were the same as those
of the infantry, for they would often dismount from
their horses and fight on foot.

Their war-chariots were adorned with beautiful
carvings, and were guided by the flower of the
nobility. They were furnished with enormous hooks
and scythes, which spread death around as they were
driven at terrific speed through the ranks of the foe.

The plain was surrounded by carts and wagons in
which, according to the Celtic custom, were placed
the wives and daughters of the warriors who animated them with their cries, and who tended the
wounded that were brought to them from the field
of blood.

In the midst of this army there was a woman
standing in a chariot, clothed in a mantle, with a gold
chain round her neck, her face grave and stern, her
yellow hair falling to the ground.

It was Queen Boadicea, who with her two daughters by her side, had come to die or to be revenged.

With a royal dignity sublime in its shamelessness,
she showed them her body covered with sore and
ignoble stripes; with a trembling hand she pointed

to her two daughters disgraced and defiled; with a
loud and fierce voice she reminded them of their
victories, and prayed to God to complete their work
of vengeance.

" Ye Britons, she cried, are wont to fight under
the conduct of a woman, but now I ask ye not to
follow me because I am descended from illustrious
ancestors, nor because my kingdom has been stolen
from me. I ask ye to avenge me as a simple woman
who has been whipped with rods, and whose daughters have been ravished before her eyes. These
Romans are insatiable, they respect neither the age
of our fathers, nor the virginity of our daughters.
They tax our bodies; they tax our very corpses.
And what are they? They are not men. They
bathe in tepid water, live on dressed meats, drink
undiluted wine, anoint themselves with spikenard
and repose luxuriously. They are far inferior to us.
Dread them not. They must have shade and shelter,
pounded corn, wine and oil, or they perish. While
to us every herb and root is food, every juice is oil,
every stream wine, every tree a house. Come then,
remember your past victories, remember the causes
of this war, and you will understand that the day is
come when you must either conquer or die. Such
at least shall be a woman's lot; let those live who
desire to remain slaves." So saying, she loosed a

hare as an omen of victory from her bosom, and the Britons with wild shouts advanced upon their foe.

Suetonius cheered his veterans with a few emphatic words, and showed them with contempt the wild and disorderly multitude which poured confusedly towards them. He bid the trumpets sound and the troops advance.

Then arose a terrible struggle—a nation fighting for its freedom—an army fighting for its fame.

Alas! that sea of blood, that dreadful apparition, those figures in the sand were omens of Britain's downfall. Four-score thousand of its proudest warriors were slain; their wives and daughters were butchered, and Boadicea overcome with sorrow and disgrace, destroyed herself with poison.

.   .   .   .

Thus ends the reign of the Druids; the priest-kings of the North. Thus they were stripped of their crowns, and their sceptres, and their regal robes, and compelled to fly to the islands of the Irish channel and the German Sea, where they dwelt in hollow oaks and in little round stone houses, many of which still remain and are held in reverence by the simple islanders.

In Gaul the work of destruction had been completed even prior to the time of Suetonius. This beautiful religion had been proscribed by Tiberius ostensibly because it permitted human sacrifices, really because it possessed a dangerous power. This prohibition had been afterwards enforced by Claudius, and the Druids were massacred by the Romans wherever they were to be found. The priestesses of Sena were burnt by one of the ancient Dukes of Brittany.

Yet it is difficult to subroot an ancient religion by imperial edicts. The minds of men though prone to novelty will frequently return fondly to their first faiths, as the hearts of maidens creep back to former and almost forgotten loves.

In the fifth century, Druidism sprang back to life under the mighty Merlin, whose prophecies became so famous throughout Gaul and Britain, and who forms so conspicuous a character in the Arthurian romances.

But these wee drops of the *elixir vitæ* which could only animate the corpse for a brief space—which but gave vigor to the frame, and light to the eyes, as a lamp apparently extinguished will burst into flame ere it dies out for ever.

We find many decrees of Roman emperors, and canons of Christian councils in the sixth, seventh and eighth centuries against Druidism, and in the day of King Canute, the Dane, a law was made against the worship of the sun and moon, mountains, lakes, trees and rivers.

It is possible to discover many vestiges of the Druids and their religion in our times, and many peculiar analogies between their superstitions and those of other nations and of other priests.

Having related how this order of Priests emanated from the Patriarchs; how they received their idolatrous and ceremonial usuages from the Phœnicians; how they obtained a supreme power in those two countries which ere now have struggled for the possession of the world; how they were attacked and annihilated by the Roman soldiers, I shall leap over a chasm of centuries, and trace their faint footsteps in our homes, in our churches and in our household words.

BOOK THE FIFTH.

VESTIGES OF DRUIDISM.

I.

IN THE CEREMONIES OF THE CHURCH OF ROME.

THERE is no religion so pure and simple, and yet so mystic and divine as the religion of the Christians. What need is there of arguments to prove that it is derived from heaven, for what mortal mind could have conceived so grand and touching a principle, as that of a God who filled with love and pity could descend from His throne of bliss and honor to save from destruction this one poor star, this one faint mote in the vastness of His firmament.

To twelve men the dear Jesus left his precepts and commands. From the children of these men and of their disciples sprang a noble flock who, like their great Master, suffered harsh words and cruel torments, and death itself in a holy cause.

When God rewarded them by shedding peace upon the church from without, dissensions from within played Satan's work with her chastity and her love. Swords were then drawn for the first time by Christians against each other—swords which never

thence till now have been for a moment sheathed.
The Christian religion is divided into three established churches, the Church of Rome, the Church of
Greece, and the Church of England.   Besides these,
there are sects whose origins have been abuse upon
the one hand, and ambition upon the other hand, and
whose very titles it would occupy pages to enumerate.

Between the vulgar members of these three
churches burns a heathenish and diabolical hatred.
Its root is jealousy.   Each church affects to be the
only ladder to heaven, and damns all such souls as
refuse to ascend by them.

They are barbarians and place themselves in the
same scale with the tribe of the Cherokee Indians,
who firmly believe that the Black Hawks will not be
admitted to the pleasures of the happy hunting
grounds because they are not Cherokees.

Between the doctrines and ceremonies of the Greek
and Romish Churches, there are but a few delicate
and unimportant distinctions.   Yet the Patriarch of
the Church, every Holy Thursday, solemnly excom-
municates the Pope and all his followers.

The Church of England, and the Church of Rome
worship the same Christ.   Between these two
churches, as between two armies, is waged a scan-
dalous, vituperative war, and each fresh convert is a
battle won.

The Romish Church was sullied by many abuses, which authorized a schism and a separation among its members. Since many of those plague-spots still remain, it is right that this separation should continue.

But a dark and dangerous heresy has long been creeping silently into the heart of our religion, and converting its ministers into false vipers who, warmed and cherished by the bosom of this gentle church, use their increasing strength in darting black poison through all her veins.

They wish to transmit to our church those papist emblems and imagery, those ceremonies and customs which are harmless in themselves, but which by nourishing superstition elevate the dangerous power of the priests.

We can at present be proud of our priesthood. They constitute a body of pious, honorable, hard-working men. It is because they can exercise no undue power. Give them supreme power, and they will be Neros who will fasten us with iron chains, and murder us if we disobey them.

The priesthood of the Druids stands almost alone in the history of the past. It was directed by men, with minds elevated by philosophy and learned in the human heart. But read the religious history of other nations, and you will discover how frightfully the power of the priests has been abused.

The priests invented a thousand Gods; the priests told a thousand lies; the priests instituted a thousand absurd and horrible customs. Who first taught nations to be idolaters, to be murderers but the priests. Who instituted the festival of the Juggernaut, the Inquisition, the massacre of St. Bartholomew, but the priests.

Calvin, a priest of the Reformation, ordered his victims to be burnt with green wood—a truly Christian refinement of cruelty!

Aaron, a priest, manufactured a golden calf and taught the Jews to insult their God. And it was Caiaphas, a high priest, who committed that murder of which the more virtuous heathen Pilate washed his hands.

Look everywhere, look everywhere, and you will see the priests reeking with gore. They have converted popular and happy nations into deserts, and have made our beautiful world into a slaughter house drenched with blood and tears.

Englishmen! they are planting images, they are performing ceremonies in your houses of worship which you find it impossible to understand. They are hidden from your eyes by a dark veil; it is the veil of a Pagan goddess; it is the veil of Isis.

I would not raise this veil, and disclose the heathen origin of emblems and ceremonies which so many sanctify and revere, were it not to answer some good purpose.

I write then in the hope that the church may be preserved in its simplicity—and its priesthood in that honor and integrity which now, as a body, they possess to an extent unequalled in any instance that the priest-history of the past or the present can afford. It is indeed seldom that an English clergyman becomes a wolf clothed in lamb-skin, and preys upon his flock under words and looks of religion.

But we know that power presents temptations, which minds fortified only by three years education at a college are often unable to resist.

.   .   .   .

Before letters were invented, symbols were necessary to form a language; and it is still an argument of the Greek and Romish Churches that pictures and images are the books of those who cannot read.

They say also that since man is not a disembodied spirit like the angels, it is also impossible that he can worship the Deity with his heart alone. And it cannot be denied that dim and shadowy lights, sweet perfumes, majestic processions and strains of music will elevate the soul towards God and prepare the mind to receive heavenly and sublime impressions.

Without objecting to the use of such aids to devotion, I wish to guard people from attaching a peculiar sanctity to the bare aids in themselves, which is nothing less than idolatry. This I can best prevent by showing them how they first came into a Christian Church. And in doing so, I shall depart little from the original design of this chapter which is to investigate the vestiges of Druidism in the ceremonies of the Roman Catholic Religion.

Not only the ceremonies, but also the officers and many of the doctrines of the Church of Rome may be traced to heathen sources.

The Pope of Rome exactly resembles the Secular High-Priest of ancient Rome, and in Latin his title is the same—*Pontifex Maximus*. The office was probably an imitation of that of the Arch-Druid, who, as I have described, had supreme power over secular as well as ecclesiastical affairs, and who was surrounded by a Senate of the Chief Druids, as the Pontifex Maximus was by *Flamines*, and the Pope by Cardinals.

The distinguishing sign of the *flamen* was a HAT; and "the cardinal's hat" is a European proverb.

The Arch-Druid held his foot to be kissed on certain occasions by the common people. Julius Cæsar who had observed this custom, on being made Pontifex Maximus, compelled Pompey to do the same; in this he was followed by Caligula and Heliogabalus, whom the Pope also has wisely imitated.

The tonsure of the Romish priests is the same as
that of the priests of Isis whose heads were shaved,
a practice forbidden by God: (*Levit. xx. I. Ezek.
xliv.* 20).

Their celibacy is also heathenish.   Origen when
emasculated himself, only imitated the Hierophantes
of Athens who drank an infusion of hemlock to
render themselves impotent.   St. Francis who, when
tempted with carnality, would throw himself naked
on the snow making balls which he applied to his
body calling them his maid and his wife, did but
copy Diogenes who lived in a tub—a cloak, his
covering—a wallet, his kitchen—the palm of his
hand, his bottle and cup; who in the searching heat
of summer would lie naked on the hot gravel, and
in the harshest frost would embrace stone statues
covered with snow.

Plato, Pythagoras, Heraclitus, Democritus and
Zeno, the prince of Stoics, imposed celibacy upon
their disciples.   The priests of Cybele, the Mega-
byzes of Ephesus and the priests of Egypt maintained
the vow of chastity.   Eneas (*Æneid lib vi.*) in passing through the infernal regions saw no priests there
but such as had passed their lives in celibacy.

It need not be proved that there were many hermits and orders of monks among the heathen.   Even
the begging friars of the Romish church are not

original.   There was a tribe of lazy mendicant priests among the heathens, against whom Cicero wrote in his Book of Laws, who used to travel from house to house with sacks on their backs, and which were gradually filled with eatables by the superstition of their hosts.

Pythagoras established an order of nuns over whom he placed his daughter.   The Roman vestals were nuns who took a vow of chastity, and who, like Christian nuns that we have heard of, were punished with death if they disgraced it.

There was a sisterhood of Druidesses at Kildare in Ireland, whose office it was, like the Roman Vestals, to preserve a holy fire ever burning.   They devoted themselves to the service of Brighit, the Goddess of Poetry, of Physics, and of Smiths, and who is spoken of in the old Irish MSS. as the *Presiding Care*.   When Druidism was abolished, these priestesses became Christian nuns, and Brighit became St. Bridget, the tutelary saint of Ireland.   The fire was still preserved in honor of this Christian saint, and though extinguished once by the Archbishop of London, was relighted and only finally extinguished at the suppression of the monasteries in the reign of King Henry the Eighth.

The dress and ornaments of the Romish priest are borrowed from the heathens.   The Phœnician priests wore surplices. Lambskin was worn by the Persian priests. The *pelt*, which the canons wear with the fur outward, is a memorial of the custom of the early heathens, who having killed the beasts for sacrifice, flayed them and taking the skins put them over their head with the fur outwards. On the *saccos*, or episcopal garment of the Russian bishops are suspended small silver bells, which were also worn on the robes of the priests of Persia and of the High-Priest of the Jews.

The *crosier*, or pastoral staff of the Pope was also used by the Druids, and answers to the *lituus* of the Roman augurs and the *hieralpha* of the Hindoos.

The Arch-Druid wore bands precisely resembling those which the Romish and English clergy wear now, and which a short time ago the students of our universities were compelled to wear in their public examinations.

Votive offerings and pilgrimages are known by all to be of Pagan extraction.

The fasts, penances and self-tortures of the Romish priests find a parallel among the Yogees or Gymnosophists of India, who wandered about the world naked as they had been born, sometimes standing on one leg on the burning sands—passing weeks without nourishment, years without repose—exposed to the sun, to the rain, to the wind—standing with their arms crossed above their heads till the sinews shrank and their flesh withered away—fixing their eyes upon the burning sun till their moisture was seared and their light extinguished.

When a Brahmin became a grandfather he gave up the management of his affairs to his son, and quitted the city for the desert, the company of men for eternal solitude. He dressed in the bark of trees; he was not permitted to wear linen nor to cut his nails. He bathed nine times a day; he read and meditated ever on the Holy Vedas. At night alone he slept, and then on the bare ground. In the summer months he sat in the full blaze of the sun, surrounded by four fires; in the four months of rain, he dwelt in a stage raised above the water by four poles but unroofed; during the four winter months he sat all night in the cold water.

And always performing the fast of Chanderayan.

Soon his spirits would sink, and tired of life he was allowed to commit suicide, which was considered the sure passport to heaven. Some burn themselves, some drowned themselves, some flung themselves from precipices, and some walked, walked, walked till they dropped down dead.

The fast of Chanderayan consisted in eating one mouthful a day, and increasing a mouthful every day for a month, and then decreasing a mouthful every day for the same length of time.   A tribe of the Egyptian priests fasted perpetually, abstaining from eggs which they considered liquid meat, and from milk which they esteemed a kind of blood.

The members of the Greek Church are more scrupulous than those of Rome, for they will not eat eggs or fish when fasting.

The religious rites of the Romish Church are closely assimilated to those of the heathens.

In the *Dibaradané*, or offering-of-fire, the officiating Brahmin always rang a small bell.   Also the women-of-the-idol, the dancing girls of the Indian pagodas had golden bells attached to their feet.

The wax tapers which are constantly kept burning in Roman Catholic churches remind us of the practice of most of the ancient nations who preserved fires continually burning in their temples; for instance in the pagodas of the Brahmins; in the sanctuaries of Jupiter Ammon; in the Druidic temple at Kildare; in the Capitol at Rome; and in the temple of the Gaditanian Hercules at Tyre.

The Egyptians used lamps in the celebration of their religious services.   They had one festival which they called *The Feast of Lamps*, which they used to celebrate by sailing down the Nile to the temple of Isis at Sais by torchlight.   Those who were unable to attend, lighted the lamps, which were small cups filled with salt and oil, and a lighted wick floated within.

It is curious that this Pagan observance should be still preserved by the Papists. A few years ago I was in the house of a Roman Catholic at vesper time. " I cannot attend vespers to-day," he said, " so I do this." And he fetched a glass saucer which was filled with oil, and lighted a wick which was floating in the midst. After some few minutes the light died out, " Now," said he, " vespers are over."

The Persians used a kind of holy water which was named *zor*. But it is needless to produce such instances. Water, as a principle of generation, and as one of the four elements was revered by all heathendom. The very *aspersoire* or sacred waterpot which the ancient Romans used for their temple, may be found among the implements of their successors.

Their turnings and genuflexions are copied from the *deisuls* of the Druids. The Druidic religious dances which were performed in a circle, in imitation of the revolution of the heavenly bodies, are preserved to posterity by the cardinals who advance to the Pope in a circle, by the Turkish dervishes, and by the French and English peasantry in various rural dances.

The heathens were not without their liturgies.

The Persians used a long form of prayer for the ceremony of marriage, and the use of the ring on the third finger of the left hand was known to all the ancients as Tertullian himself admits. In the Greek Church of Russia the couple are crowned with garlands which are removed on the eighth day. This, an ancient Roman observance, is not a traditional superstition of the Russians, but a ceremony authorized by their religion, and a service in their liturgy. The veil which our brides wear is also a remnant of ancient Rome.

> ———Dudum sedet illa parato
> Flammeolo.—*Juv. Sat. X.*

As is also the superstition among Papist that it is unlucky to marry in the month of May. Ovid records it in a distich.

> Nec viduæ tædis eadem nec virginis apta
> Tempora. Quæ nupsit non diuturna fuit.
> Hac quoque de causâ si te proverbia tangunt
> Mense malas Maio nubere vulgus ait.

Our funeral practice of throwing three handfuls of earth on the coffin, and saying : *earth to earth, ashes to ashes, dust to dust,* was in use among the ancient Egyptians, and our mutes resemble the hired mourners of all the ancient nations.

The Vedas are full of exorcisms against those evil spirits which, as the Hindoos supposed, crowded about the sacrifice and impeded the religious rites.

There are forms of exorcism used by Romish priests, and in the first liturgy of Edward VI, there was a form of exorcism in the baptismal service which since has been erased.

The Romans used to consecrate their temples, when first built, with prayers and sacrifices, and sprinklings of holy water.

The mass is acknowledged by the Catholic priests to be a sacrificial service, and the host made of wheat flour is an exact imitation of the consecrated cakes which were used by the heathens.

The ancient Persians carried their infants to the temple a few days after they were born, and presented them to the priest who stood before the holy fire in the presence of the burning sun.   He took the child and plunged it into a vase full of water for the purification of its soul.   After which it was anointed, received the sign of the cross, and was fed with milk and honey.

Such is the origin of infant baptism, of the font, and of the ceremony of signing the forehead with the figure of the cross—none of which are derived from God or from His Holy Scriptures.

When the child had arrived at the age of fifteen years, the priest invested him with the robe called *Sudra* and with the girdle, and initiated him into the mysteries of their religion.

This is plainly the same as the Christian confirmation, before which the church does not permit us to receive the sacrament.

We first hear of the sacramental offering of bread and wine as used by Melchisedek. I have described it among the ceremonies of Druidism. Among the Hebrews it was called *qum* whence our word "communion."

I have now to consider the great symbol of the Christian religion—the cross. Were it regarded as a mere emblem of our Lord's suffering I should be silent upon the matter; but since it is an object of actual idolatry in the Roman Catholic church, and threatens to become the same in our own, I must endeavor to correct the abuse by exposing its Pagan origin.

This cross which the Roman Catholics worship on Good Friday by taking off their shoes and approaching it on their knees, and reverently kissing it, was once as common a symbol among Pagans as the circle, the serpent or the bull.

In Ezekiel, IX. 4—6, we read that God directed the six destroyers to kill all whom they found in the city of Jerusalem, except those on whose forehead the *Taw* was inscribed. This letter *Taw* is the last in the Hebrew alphabet, and according to its ancient method of writing, exactly resembles a cross, as St. Jerome remarked 1400 years ago.

The *crux ansata* of the Egyptians, according to Ruffinus and Sozomen, was hieroglyphic, and imparted the time that was to come.

The ☿ was a phallic emblem in Egypt. Thereby also the Syrians and Phœnicians represented the planet Venus. On some of the early coins of the latter nation, we find the cross attached to a chaplet of beads placed in a circle so as to form a rosary, such as the Lamas of Thibet and China, the Hindoos and the Roman Catholics now tell over as they pray.

On a Phœnician medal discovered by Dr. Clarke in the ruins of Citium, are inscribed the cross, the rosary and the lamb.

𐤀 𐤓 † were the monograms of Osiris, Venus and Jupiter Ammon.

ᚠ ᛏ of the Scandinavian Teutates or Tuisco.

The Vaishnavas of India mark one of their idols with crosses, thus 卐 and with triangles ✡

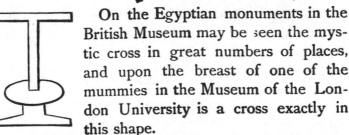

On the Egyptian monuments in the British Museum may be seen the mystic cross in great numbers of places, and upon the breast of one of the mummies in the Museum of the London University is a cross exactly in this shape.

The two principal pagodas of India, those of Benares and Mathura are built in the form of a cross. The Mexican temples are built in the form of a cross and face the four cardinal points.

Crosses have been discovered on the Scandinavian "Mark" stones in the Scottish Isles, and there are many ancient monuments in Great Britain which, but for the cross engraved upon them, would be considered Druidical.

That the Druids, like the aborigines of America and the ancient conjurers of Lapland, revered the form of the cross can hardly be doubted. *Schedius de Mor. Germ.* informs us that it was their custom to seek studiously for an oak tree large and handsome, growing up with two principal arms in the form of a cross beside the main stem. If the two horizontal arms were not sufficiently adapted to the figure, they fastened a cross beams to it. Then they consecrated it by cutting upon the right branch in fair characters the word *Hesus*, upon the middle stem, the word *Taranis*, upon the left branch *Belenus*, and over them the word *Thau*.

The tree so inscribed, they would make their Kebla like the Jewish Jerusalem, the Turk's Mecca, and the Christian's altar to which they would direct their faces when they prayed.

I can best explain the adoration of this symbol by deriving it from that constellation *The Southern Cross*, which appears only in tropical skies and which perhaps the heathens, attracted by its beauty, learned to worship, as they worshipped the sun for its God-like grandeur, and the moon for its beneficent light. The idolatry of the Roman Catholics is not confined to emblems. They have deified martyrs and other holy men, and render them a worship that is only due to God.

It is true that they draw a distinction between the adoration which they pay to God, and the homage which they pay to Saints, calling the one in the language of the schools *Latria*, from γατζεια the worship due to God only, and the latter *Dulia*, from δουλεια an inferior kind of worship. But this distinction is too delicate for the illiterate to understand.

A plurality of Gods I have shown to be one of the abuses of ancient heathenism. In this abuse, they have been imitated by the modern idolaters of Rome, not only in the abstract but in the concrete: there is not only assimilation, but a reproduction.

The Romans ridiculed the Gods of Egypt whom they themselves adored but under different names. They burnt Serapis, Anubis, and Isis; they revered Pluto, Mercury and Ceres.

So the Roman Catholics while pretending to abjure the Gods of heathenism have actually adopted many of them.

The petty divinities of the Pagans were deified men, and were intercessors with Osiris, Zeus or

Jupiter, as the canonized saints of the Catholic Church are with the God of the Christians.

The Chaldees divided the year into twelve months with an angel over each month. The saints perform the same office in the Romish Calendar, and in several of the Greek churches there are twelve pictures for the twelve months representing the twelve principal saints.

The *divi*, or inferior Gods of the Romans worked miracles; altars were erected in their honor with lights continually burning before them; their relics were worshipped; convents were formed of religious men and women who took the name of *divus* or inferior God, to whom they devoted themselves, such as the Quirinals from Quirinus or Romulus; the Martiales from Mars; the Vulcanates from Vulcan. So also the Augustines from Augustine; the Franciscans from Francis; the Dominicans from Dominic.

The Roman *divi* were tutelary Gods over various vocations—as Neptune over mariners—Pan over shepherds—Pales over husbandmen—Flora over courtezans—Diana over huntsmen. So the seamen, among Catholics, pray to St. Nicholas—the shepherds to St. Windoline—the husbandmen to St. John the Baptist—the courtezans to St. Magdalene—and the huntsmen to St. Hubert.

The saints too have received the equipage of the

divi. To St. Wolfgang, the hatchet or hook of Saturn—to Moses, the horns of Jupiter Ammon—to St. Peter, the keys of Janus.

In the same way as the Pagans worshipped these *divi* but stigmatized them—Apollo as a rake, Mercury as an arrant thief, and Venus as a courtezan; there are things recorded by pious Catholics themselves of those Popes which are infallible and of saints which are said to be in heaven, quite as little to their credit.

Minutius Felix jeers the Pagans for the vile drudgery they have put upon their Gods. "Sometimes," says he, "Hercules is set to empty dung; Apollo turns cow-herd to Ametus; Neptune hires himself to Laomedon as bricklayer to build up the walls of Troy, and is cheated out of his wages."

So among the glorious miracles of the Holy Virgin, we find that she descends from heaven to bleed a young man in the arm; to take the place of a naughty abbess who has eloped with a monk; to mend the gown of St. Thomas of Canterbury who had torn it on a nail, and to wipe the sweat off the faces of the monks of Chevraux whilst they were at work.

But as I have said before, there has been something more than imitation. There has been adoption. The Roman Catholics have canonized several of the

Pagan gods. Bacchus, the God of topers, has become St. Baccus, a worshipful saint of the perennial calendar; and Brighit, the Goddess of the Druids, St. Bridget, a patron saint of Ireland.

The most distinguishing feature of the Roman Catholic religion is the idolatrous worship of the Virgin Mary. It is idolatrous, for to this woman whom it is palpable from Scripture that Christ treated as a being inferior to himself, are rendered prayers and honors as numerous and high as those which are rendered to Him, and in all instances they are placed upon a level with each other.

They have made her immaculate, although she was the wife of a carpenter, and although the brethren of Jesus are more than once mentioned in the gospels.

And as there was no mention made in Scripture of her death, they inferred that, like Enoch and Elijah and her Holy Son, she had been taken up into Heaven. Upon this bare conjecture, the doctrine was assiduously inculcated into the minds of the ignorant, and a service was introduced into the liturgy called " The Assumption of the Virgin Mary."

Bonaventura who was canonized a saint, and who is spoken of by his brother-catholics as the Seraphic Doctor, wrote a book called " The Imitation of the

Virgin Mary," after St. Thomas-a-Kempis' well-known work, in which he exhorts all faithful catholics to pray to the Virgin Mary by whose intercession their souls may be saved.

In the Psalter which St. Bonaventura edited, he changes in each of the 150 Psalms the word Lord or God, for that of Lady or Mary, interspersing in some much of his own composition, and adding the Gloria Patri to each.

For instance in the 148th Psalm—(*page* 491 *of the Psalter*).

"Praise our Lady of Heaven, glorify her in the highest.   Praise her all ye men and cattle, ye birds of the heaven and fishes of the sea.   Praise her sun and moon, ye stars and circles of the planets.   Praise her Cherubin and Seraphin, thrones and dominions and powers.   Praise her all ye legions of angels. Praise her all ye orders of spirits on high.

"Let everything that hath breath praise our Lady."

Theophilus Raynaud, a Jesuit of Lyons, in his work entitled *Diptycha Mariana* thus writes:—

"The torrents of Heaven and the fountains of the great deep, I would rather open than close in homage of the Virgin. *And if her son Jesus has omitted anything as to the pre-eminence of the exaltation of his own mother*, I a servant, I a slave, not indeed with

effect, but with affection would delight in filling
it up."

Again:—

"In like manner are her feet to be blessed with
which she carried the Lord, the womb in which she
carried him, the heart whence she courageously believed in him and fervently loved him, the breasts
with which she gave him suck, the hands with which
she nourished him, the mouth and tongue with which
she gave to him the happy kisses of our redemption,
the nostrils with which she smelled the sweet-smell-
ing fragrance of his humanity, the ears with which
she listened with delight to his eloquence, the eyes
with which she devoutly looked upon him, the body
and soul which Christ consecrated in her with every
benediction.   And these most sacred members must
be saluted and blessed with all devotion, so that
separate salutations must be addressed to the several
members separately, namely, *Hail Mary!* two to
the feet, one to the womb, one to the heart, two to
the breasts, two to the hands, two to the mouth and
tongue, two to the lips, two to the nostrils, two to
the ears, two to the eyes, two to the soul and body.
And thus in all there are twenty salutations which
after the manner of a daily payment with separate
and an equal number of kneelings, if it can be done
before her image or altar, are to be paid to the

glorious Virgin according to that psalm, (144). Every day will I give thanks unto thee and praise THY name for ever and ever."

In the following extract from a little work published at Dublin, 1836, and entitled " *The Little Testament of the Holy Virgin*," God and the Virgin are placed upon an equality.

" Mary! sacred name under which no one should despair. Mary! sacred name often assaulted but always victorious. Mary! it shall be my life, my strength, my comfort. Every day shall I invoke it and the divine name of Jesus. The Son shall awake the recollection of the mother, and the mother that of the son. *Jesus and Mary!* this is what my heart shall say at my last hour if my tongue cannot. I shall hear them on my death—bed, they shall be wafted on my expiring breath, and I with them to see THEM, know THEM, bless and love THEM for eternity. Amen."

But she is sometimes made even greater than God.

" My soul," says the blessed Eric Suzon, is in the hands of Mary, so that if the Judge wishes to condemn me, the sentence must pass through this clement Queen, and she knows how to prevent its execution."

It even became a custom at one time in their

church to date the Christian era not from the birth of the Christ, but from the virgin mother of God. See Emanuel Acosta's Acts of the Jesuits in the East. Dilingæ. 1571. *Ad annum usque a Deipara Virgine*, 1568.

The question now naturally arises, why does the Virgin Mary receive this worship and these honors which are only due to God.

You will be surprised when I tell you that this also is a remnant of heathenism.

In all nations, long before the Christian era, a female with a child in her arms had been worshipped. Among the Egyptians it was Isis, among the Etruscans it was Venus, among the Phrygians it was Atys.

In fact as Isis was the original of the Proserpine, the Venus, the Diana, the Juno, the Maia and the Cere of ancient Rome, so she was the original of the Virgin Mary of the Roman Catholic Church.

In Montfaucon we find several plates of Isis giving suck to the boy Horus.

In the year 1747, a Mithraic monument was found at Oxford—a female nursing an infant—which Dr. Stukeley proved to be a representation of the Goddess of the Year nursing the God Day.

It is indeed not improbable that Oxford with its seven hills, its river Isis, and the bull in its coat or arms had been established by priests who, like the Druids, were acquainted with Egyptian lore.

An ancient Etruscan monument was discovered at Rome, the precise model of those pictures of the Madonna and her child so common in Italy and throughout the world.

In many churches on the continent, the Virgin Mary is represented with a lily or lotus in her hand. This plant was sacred to Isis, and was held in reverence by the priests of Egypt and of India.

Isis was the wife of Osiris, as the moon was called the wife of the sun.

In the hymn of the Assumption, the Virgin is entreated "to calm the rage of her heavenly husband."

The month of May was sacred to Isis.

It is called by the Papists " *Mary's month*."

Venus, the Isis of the Romans, was born from the foam of the sea.

In the form of prayer called *Litaniæ Lauritanæ*, there are more than forty addresses to the Virgin, invoking her as the star of the sea, as the mystical rose, and by a variety of other heathen epithets.

In another prayer she is named *amica stella, naufragis*, and in Sanval's Historie des Antiquités de Paris, *étoile éclatante de la mer*.

The chief title of Venus was *Regina Cæloium.*

And the Holy Virgin is repeatedly invoked in the Romish liturgy as the Queen of Heaven.

Finally, on the 25th of March the ancient Phrygians devoted a festival to the mother of the Gods, which very day still bears among Catholics and their Protestant imitators the name of Lady's Day.

All this does not impeach one iota or tittle of the truth of Christianity. I do not say that the Christians invented a personage, and called her the Virgin Mary. I merely prove that the Roman Catholics pay those idolatrous tributes to the Virgin Mary which their ancestors rendered to Isis in Egypt, or to Venus in Rome, and that they represent her in the same manner.

For instance, in the pictures of the Madonna and the Child, we see the Virgin's head encircled by a crescent halo of light, and the child's by many luminous rays.

The one is a symbol of the new moon sacred to Isis, the latter an imitation of the radiance of the sun of whom Horus was the offspring.

The spires and towers of our churches are also imitated from the pyramids and obelisks of antiquity. These were erected as emblems of the sun's beams which fall pyramidically upon the earth.

Many of the heathen festivals are still celebrated by Christians. In the liturgy of the Greek Church there is a ritual named "The Benediction of the Waters." A wooden temple, richly gilt and hung round with sacred pictures, is erected upon the Neva at St. Petersburg when it is frozen, and a procession is formed by the clerks, the deacons, the priests and the bishops dressed in their richest robes, and bearing the tapers and the sacred pictures, and the service is read within the temple.

This is not unlike "The Feast of Lamps" before described, which the Egyptians partly celebrated on the Nile, a river which in one of the prayers of the Greek Church is called "The Monarcn of the Floods."

The conception of the Virgin Mary is represented on the same day (the 2nd of February) as that of the miraculous conception of Juno by the ancient Romans. This, says the author of the Perennial Calendar, is a remarkable coincidence.

It is also a remarkable coincidence that the Feast of All-Saints, which is celebrated by the Roman Catholics on the 2nd of November and which retains its place in the Protestant calendar, should have been on the same day as the *Festum dei Mortis* of the Romans, and should still be annually kept by the Buddhists of Thibet, and by the natives of South America and as a Druidic custom by the rustic classes of Ireland.

It is also a remarkable coincidence that the Romans should have had their *Prosipernalia*, or Feast of Candles or Candlemass in February—their *Palelia*, or shepherd's feast on Midsummer Day which is sacred to St. John the Baptist, and that the Romish Carnival should be held at the same time as the ancient Saturnalia, and should resemble so closely those orgies which were of a masquerade character.

Thus we see that the Roman Catholics have been in the habit of celebrating Christian festivals upon days which were held sacred by the heathens. Whether this was from mere slavish imitation, or from a fondness for old associations, or from a desire to sanctify those days unhallowed by paganism it is impossible to say.

One of the most extraordinary examples of this custom is to be found in our grand festival of Christmas.

All will allow, I think, that there is no evidence to prove that the twenty-fifth of December was the actual day upon which Christ was born. And that He really arose on Easter Day can scarcely be believed, since the fixing of that day was not arranged among the early Christians till after swords as well as words had been used in the conflict, and several fierce battles had been fought.

I hope that I shall not weaken the genial feelings

with which Christmas Day, that holiday of the year, is greeted by the nation if I expose the real origin of the festival. But that I feel sure is impossible. It would need something more than a few facts from old books to blot out all those happy associations which crowd around that glorious festival, which though it may be celebrated on the wrong day is kept in the right manner.

I may, however, show those Christians who worship the letter and not the spirit, who attach more sanctity to the day than to the festival, who set their children over grave books and who forbid them to laugh on that day when there is a smile even on the poor man's lips, I may show those word-mongers, those silly Puritans, those harsh blunderers in religion what honor they have paid to heathenism all their lives.

The festival of the twenty-fifth of December, which we call Christmas, was observed by the Druids on that day by lighting great fires on the tops of hills. The festival was repeated on the twelfth day afterwards, which we call old Christmas Day.

And even now there are certain rites performed under the sacred mistletoe on Christmas Day which certainly have little to do with Christianity.

The Jews also celebrated a festival on the twenty-fifth of December which they called ϑως or the feast of light, and which Josephus believed to have been instituted by Judas Maccabæus.

The twenty-fifth of December too was the birthday of the God Mithra, and it was an old custom of the heathens to celebrate the birthdays of their Gods.

And now I will explain when this day was first established as the birthday of Christ. The Cœnobite monks finding that in their monasteries (most of which were pagan seminaries built efore the Christian era) a day had been from time immemorial dedicated to the God Sol as his birthday, and that he bore the name of *Lord*—this *Lord* they conceived must be their Lord, and after many disputes the twenty-fifth of December was established as the anniversary of Christ, and so the Druidic festival of the winter solstice became a Christian ceremony.

The origin of *Sunday* is very similar; but while the heathen festival of Christmas has received a Christian name, this has retained its Pagan appellation.

Such was the abhorrence which the early Christians felt for their persecutors, the Jews, that they were wont to reject all that was Jewish, as the first Puritans rejected all that was Romish without considering its intrinsic merits.

God had ordained the seventh day for man's rest

and recreation.   He had given forth that edict from
Mount Sinai not to the Israelites only, but to the
whole world.   But since the Jews faithfully kept this
commandment, the Christians hated the Sabbath and
took a step which was wholly unauthorized by their
Master, or by any of his Apostles.   They changed
the day.

They called this new day the Lord's Day, or the
Day-of-the-Sun.

The word *Lord* is heathen, and is equivalent to
Baal in Chaldee and to Adonis in Phœnician.   It
first crept into the Scripture thus:

The Jews, in obedience to the law " thou shalt not
take the name of Jehovah thy God in vain," never
wrote or spoke His name except on the most solemn
occasions.   And the first translators to avoid the
frequent repetition of the word, first used this hieroglyphic and afterwards the term which the
Pagans applied to their God Sol, which in Greek
was πνριος in Latin *dominus*, in Celtic *adon*, in
Hebrew *adoni*.

Now the Persians set apart every month four of
these Lord's days or lesser festivals to the Sun.   On
these days, they had more solemn service in their
temples than on other days, reading portions of their
sacred books and preaching morality.

But the most curious point of resemblance is that

on these days alone they prayed *standing*.   And in the sixteenth canon of the Council of Nice to kneel in prayer on Sundays is forbidden.

Constantine, after pretending to be converted to Christianity, ordered the day *Domini invicti Solis* to be set apart for the celebration of peculiar mysteries in honor of the great god Sol.

The early Christians were accused by the heathens of worshipping the sun, and Justin, as if loathing the very name of the Jewish Sabbath, preferred writing of it as μнеσa τον ἡλις the day-of-the-sun.

Since it would be now almost impossible to restore our weekly day of rest to that day which God thought fit to appoint, and which man thought fit to alter, I may be blamed for having made these disclosures which certainly do not redound to the honor of our religion.

But I have had my reason.   It is to show the folly of those who go word-mongering, to make triumphant comparisons between the Day-of-the-sun as observed by Christians, and God's Sabbath as observed by Jews; who bring out their religion, their consciences, their bibles, their sternest faces and their best clothes upon this day, and who believe or seem to believe that God sleeps all the week, and that if they go to church on Sunday they succeed in deceiving him.

It is not at this hour or at that hour that God is to be worshipped. Lip-services resemble the treacherous kisses of a Judas, and the heart does not naturally aspire towards heaven at the striking of a clock or at the ringing of a church bell.

Before concluding this chapter, I should wish to exculpate myself from the supposition that I have written in an unjust spirit against the members of the Roman Catholic Church.

I know that they can boast of many devout disciples—of many enterprising missionaries—of many conscientious priests. I know that they are not now more foolish and bigoted than the members of the Protestant churches, as in former times the murderers of St. Bartholomew were no worse than the cruel Calvin, nor Bloody Mary than James the First. In those days a remnant of the horrible custom of human sacrifice was preserved by all alike. They martyred those of the same religion as themselves but not of the same sect, burning them, drowning them, tearing them limb from limb like the Pagans of old, as offerings to a kind and gracious God.

It is true that the Roman Catholics were the most ruthless in barbarity and the most ingenious in torture, but it was because they possessed the most power.

I know that Roman Catholic priests do not really

worship those images of the saints to which they bend their knees. But though they are not idolaters themselves, it cannot be denied that they have taught their disciples to be idolaters.

I do not suppose that men of genius or even of education ever yet were, or ever could be image-worshippers.

Listen to these words of the Emperor Julian, written in an age that is supposed to have been enslaved in idolatry :

" *The statues of the gods, the altars that are raised to them, and the holy fires that are burnt in their honor have been instituted by our fathers as signs and emblems of the presence of the Gods, not that we should regard them as Gods, but that we should honor the Gods in them.*"

I might quote fifty other passages to prove that in all idolatrous nations the priests and philosophers, though affecting to be image-worshippers, have in their hearts scorned those pieces of wood and stone to which their dupes so devoutly kneeled.

In papistry, there are as many dupes and as much idolatry as ever existed in Egypt, in Italy, or in Greece.

Witness a Roman Catholic service, and you will see heads bowed before stone-images and prayers, murmured not in mere reverence but in actual adoration.

Study the doctrine of Transubstantiation.   Is not that an instance of the emblem being forgotten in the God?

These abuses are melancholy to contemplate, for these alone it is which hold two Christian churches asunder.   These with the Platonic dogma of purgatory upon which no man can decide, and upon which therefore it is foolish for man to contend.

English priests beware how you nurse idolatry; for those who do so, enchain not only others but themselves.

In the reign of Peter the Great, a law was passed by a synod of the Greek Church in Russia enacting that the use of pictures in churches was contrary to the principles in Christianity, and that all such should be removed from places of worship.

The Emperor sanctioned this law, but feared to put it into execution lest it should cause a general insurrection.

Superstition, born of Satan, fed and fostered by priests, like a hideous cuttle-fish has cast its white and slimy arms around the Harlot of Babylon, and has bedaubed her with its black blood.   Now she loves this blood and knows not that it defiles her; she loves these embraces and knows not that they enslave her.   But some day aspiring to be free, she will attempt to rise from her grave of sand and foul weeds; and then seizing her in its horrible arms, that demon who so long has triumphed over her will sink with her forever beneath the waves.

II.

IN THE EMBLEMS OF FREEMASONRY.

THERE is a divine and hidden science whose origin can only be discovered by the wavering lights of tradition, whose doctrines and purposes are enveloped in sacred mysteries.

It is now degenerated into a society of gluttons and wine-bibbers, who yawn while their Masters expound to them those emblems which have excited the wonder of the greatest philosophers of the past, and who deem that the richest gem of freemasonry is the banquet which closes the labor of the Lodge.

And yet this order can boast of some learned and intellectual men, who endeavor to find the key to the hidden language of symbols, and who appreciate at its true value the high honors which the initiated are permitted to enjoy.

In spite of the abuses with which it has been degraded, in spite of the sneers with which the ignorant revile it, this institution still possesses much that is holy and sublime.

No feelings can be compared with those which a young man feels when, attired in strange array, blind-folded, the dagger pointed to his naked left breast, he is led through the mystic labyrinth, whose intricate ways are emblematical of the toilsome wanderings of his soul.

The strains of solemn music—the mysterious words—the low knock at the portal—the sudden blaze of light—and the strange sight which await his eyes feeble and fluttering from their long imprisonment.

What awe he feels, as kneeling on his right knee, his left hand placed upon the Book of the Law, encircled by the Masters in their robes of office, and the two white wands held over his head in the form of a cross, he takes the oath of secrecy and faith, "to hail, conceal and never reveal the hidden mysteries of the fellowship" to which he is now admitted.

And what pride flushes in his heart when the secret signs and key-words are imparted to him, and when the white apron, a badge more glorious than the fabled Golden Fleece, or the Roman Eagle is tied round his waist.

Surrounded by all those signs and symbols by which the ancient nations were wont to express the power and presence of God, the Mason's Lodge resembles a scene of enchantment in the midst of this wilderness which we call the world.   And those who are thus assembled together in mystic robes, seem spirits of another age, who have returned to hold their hidden meetings once more in the catacombs of the Egyptian pyramids, or in the cavern-temples sacred to Mithra, or in the subterranean labyrinths of the holy Druids.

The brethren seated in a circle, one of the Masters arises and advances to the midst.   He relates to them a tradition of the origin of their craft.

" After the sun had descended down the seventh age from Adam before the flood of Noah, there was born unto Methusael, the son of Mehujael, a man called Lamach who took unto himself two wives. the name of the one was Adah, of the other Zillah. Now Adah his first wife, bare two sons—the one named Jabel and the other Jubal.   Jabal was the inventor of geometry and the first who built houses of stone and timber, and Jubal was the inventor of music and harmony.   Zillah, his second wife, bare Tubal Cain, the instructor of every artificer in brass and iron, and a daughter called Naamah who was the founder of the weaver's craft.

" All these had knowledge from above, that the Almighty would take vengeance for sin either by fire or by water, so great was the wickedness of the world. So they reasoned among themselves how they might preserve the knowledge of the sciences which they had found, and Jabal said that there were two different kinds of stone of such virtue that one would not burn and the other would not sink—the one called *marble* and the other *latres*. They then agreed to write all the science that they had found upon these stones.

" After the destruction of the world, these two pillars were discovered by Hermes, the son of Shem. Then the craft of masonry began to flourish, and Nimrod was one of the earliest patrons of the art. Abraham, the son of Jerah, was skilled in the seven sciences and taught the Egyptians the science of grammar. Euclid was his pupil, and instructed them in the art of making mighty walls and ditches to preserve their houses from the inundations of the Nile, and by geometry measured out the land, and divided it into partitions so that each man might ascertain his own property. And he it was who gave masonry the name of geometry.

" In his days, it came to pass that the sovereign and lords of the realm had gotten many sons unlawfully by other men's wives, insomuch that the land was grievously burdened with them. A council was called but no reasonable remedy was proposed. The king then ordered a proclamation to be made throughout his realms, that high rewards would be given to any man who would devise a proper method for maintaining the children.   Euclid dispelled the difficulty.   He thus addressed the king: 'My noble sovereign, if I may have order and government of these lord's sons, I will teach them the seven liberal sciences, whereby they may live honestly like gentle- men, provided that you will grant me power over them by virtue of your royal commission.'

"This request was immediately complied with, and Euclid established a Lodge of Masons."

This tale is curious as being the earliest account of an educational institution.

There are various traditions of minor interest re- lating to the patriarchal ages and to the wanderings of the Israelites in the wilderness.

The Freemasons claim descent from that body of builders who, some from Phœnicia, and some from India, came to Jerusalem to erect the temple of Solomon.   They also assert that these masons were governed by the same laws, and united by the same ties as those of the modern order, and in the initia- tion of a Master-mason the following tradition is related respecting the death of the Phœnician Hiram Abiff, the master architect who directed the building of the temple:

"There were fifteen fellow-craftsmen, who finding

that the temple was almost finished, and that they had not received the master's word because their time was not come, agreed to extort it from their master, the skilful Hiram Abiff, on the first opportunity, that they might pass for masters in other countries and have masters' wages. Twelve recanted and the other three determined to carry out the plot. Their names were Jubela, Jubelo, and Jubelum. These three crafts knowing that it was always the master's custom at twelve at noon, when the men were called off to refreshment, to go into the *sanctum sanctorum* to pray to the true and living God— they placed themselves at the three entrances to the temple, viz., at the west, south and east doors. There was no entrance in the north, because thence the sun darts no rays. Thus they waited while he made his prayer to the Lord, to have the word or grip as he came out, or his life. So Hiram came to the east door, and Jubela demanded the master's word. Hiram told him he did not receive it in such a manner but he must wait, and time and a little patience would bring him to it, for it was not in his power to deliver it except the three Grand Masters were together, viz: Solomon, King of Israel, Hiram, King of Tyre, and Hiram Abiff.

" Jubela struck him across the throat with a 24-inch gauge. He fled thence to the south door where he

was accosted in the same manner by Jubelo to whom
he gave a similar answer, and who gave him a blow
with a square upon his left breast. Hiram reeled
but recovered himself, and flew to the west door
where Jubelum gave him a heavy blow upon the
head with a common gavel or setting maul which
proved his death.

"After this they carried him out of the west door
and hid him in a heap of rubbish till it was twelve at
night, when they found means to bury him in a
handsome grave, six feet east and west, and six feet
in height.

"When Hiram was missed, King Solomon made
great inquiry after him, and not hearing anything
of him supposed him to be dead. The twelve crafts
that had recanted hearing the said report, and their
consciences pricking them, went and informed King
Solomon with white aprons and gloves as tokens of
their innocence. King Solomon forthwith sent them
in search of the three murderers who had absconded,
and they agreed to make the pursuit in four parties,
three going north, three south, three east, and three
west.

"As one of these parties traveled down to the sea
of Joppa, one of them sitting himself down to rest by
the side of a rock, heard the following lamentations
proceed from a cleft within:—

"'O that I had my throat cut across, and my tongue torn out by the root, and buried in the sands of the sea at low water a cable length from the shore, where the tide doth regularly ebb and flow twice in the course of the twenty-four hours, than that I had been concerned in the death of our master Hiram.'

"And then another voice:

"'Oh! that I had my heart torn from under my naked left breast, and given to the vultures of the air as a prey, rather than I had been concerned in the death of so good a master.'

"'But oh!' cried Jubelum. I struck him harder than you both, for I killed him. Oh! that I had had my body severed in two, one part carried to the south, and the other to the north, my bowels burnt to ashes and scattered before the four winds of the earth, rather than I had been concerned in the death of our master Hiram.'

"The brother that heard these sorrowful lamentations hailed the other two, and they went into the cleft of the rock and took them and bound them, and brought them before King Solomon, when they owned what had passed, and what they had done, and did not desire to live, therefore King Solomon ordered their own sentences to be executed upon them, saying, 'They have signed their own deaths, and let it be upon them as they have said.'

" ' Jubela was taken out, and his throat cut across, and his tongue torn out by the root, and buried in the sands of the sea at low water, a cable length from the shore, where the tide did regularly ebb and flow twice in the course of the twenty-four hours.

" Jubelo's heart was torn from under his naked left breast, and was given to the vultures of the air as a prey.

" Jubelum's body was severed in two, one part was carried to the north, the other to the south, his bowels were burnt to ashes and scattered to the four winds of the earth."

.　.　.　.　.　.　.　.

The real secret of Freemasonry, viz., its origin and purport, as yet remain an enigma and will probably ever remain so.

There are some authors who have fixed the source of this sacred and mysterious fountain within the oaken groves of the extinguished order of the Druids.

Who assert that when Druidism was proscribed, its priests adopted various disguises and carried their learning into various professions. Some became school-masters and taught science to the youth of Britain, as they had once done in the forest semin- aries of Mona. Some fortune-tellers, the parents of the tribes of gypsies who still retain a kind of brotherhood united by oaths and secret signs, and who at one time possessed so strange an ascendancy over the minds of the vulgar.

And others who formed themselves into a community resembling, if not in their power, at least in their unanimity, that ancient body of priests who had once been the sovereigns of Britain.

At first I was inclined to believe that such was really the case, and that Freemasonry was no more than a reproduction of Druidism in the Middle Ages. On searching for materials, I met with evidence *in limine* which tended to confirm me in this conviction. There was a manuscript discovered in the Bodleian Library at Oxford in 1696, which was supposed to have been written about the year 1436. It purports to be an examination of one of the brotherhood by King Henry VI, and is allowed by all masonic writers to be genuine.

Its title is as follows: "*Certain questions with answers to the same concerning the mystery of masonry written by King Henry the Sixth and faithfully copied by me John Leylande, antiquarian, by command of his highness.*"

I give an extract modernizing the English of the original, which, though quaint, would be unintelligible to all but antiquaries :—

"What mote it be?—It is the knowledge of nature, and the power of its various operations; particularly the skill of reckoning, of weights and measures, of constructing buildings and dwellings of all kinds, and the true manner of forming all things for the use of man.

"Where did it begin?—it began with the first men of the East, who were before the first men of the West, and coming with it, it hath brought all comforts to the wild and comfortless.

"Who brought it to the West?—the Phœnicians who, being great merchants, came first from the East into Phœnicia, for the convenience of commerce, both East and West by the Red and Mediterranean Seas.

"How came it into England?—Pythagoras, a Grecian, traveled to acquire knowledge in Egypt and in Syria, and in every other land where the Phœnicians had planted masonry; and gaining admittance into all lodges of masons, he learned much, and returned and dwelt in Grecia Magna, growing and becoming mighty wise and greatly renowned. Here he formed a great lodge at Crotona, and made many masons, some of whom traveled into France, and there made many more, from whence, in process of time, the art passed into England."

This, I need not remind the reader, is a story very similar to those current respecting the first planting of Druidism in Britain.

I also discovered as I thought, a key to the tradition of Hiram Abiff, which I have just related, viz., that it was simply the story of Osiris (killed by Typhon the Evil Spirit, buried in a coffin and found by Isis) so corrupted by modern Masons.

In the continuation of the story of Hiram, it is stated that the twelve crafts on discovering his body were unable to raise it, and that King Solomon ordered a lodge of master-masons to be summoned and said, "I will go myself in person and try to raise the body by *the master's grip or the lion's paw.*

By means of this grip the Grand-Master Hiram was raised.

Now in a figure painted on a mummy at the Austin Fryar's of *La Place des Victores*, representing the death and resurrection of Osiris, is seen an exact model of the position of the master-mason as he raises Hiram.

Jubela, Jubelo, Jubelum are merely variations from the Latin word *jubeo*, I command. The pretended assassins are represented as demanding the master's grip and word from Hiram in an imperious manner.

A more satisfactory proof of the truth of this statement is contained in an astronomical notion of the Hindoos, whose *Chrisna* is the same as the Osiris of the Egyptians.

The *Decans*, or *Elohim*, are the gods of whom it is said the Almighty created the Universe. They arranged the order of the zodiac. The *Elohim* of the summer were gods of a benevolent disposition: they made the days long, and loaded the sun's head with topaz. While *the three wretches* that presided in the winter at the extreme end of the year, hid in the realms below, were, with the constellation to which they belonged, cut off from the rest of the zodiac; and *as they were missing*, were consequently accused of bringing Chrisna into those troubles which at last ended in his death.

Even allowing these premises to be true, it does not necessarily follow that the traditionary account of the building of Solomon's Temple by masons was also allegorical.

And indeed there is so much that is purely Hebrew in ceremonial masonry, that one is almost forced to believe that the Freemasons of the present day are really descended from a body of architects, who, like the Dionysiacks of Asia Minor, were united into a fraternal association and who erected the temple of Solomon.

In these ceremonies, however, and in their emblems there is much also that is Druidic, and if Freemasonry did not emanate from Druidism, there can be no doubt that it sprang from the same origin.

I will trace out the affinity between the Masonic Order of the Present, and the Druid Order of the Past. It shall be for the reader to decide whether these Masonic usages are vestiges of Druidism, or mere points of family resemblance.

The initiations of Masons are so similar to those of the Druids, that any Mason reading my article upon the subject must have been struck by the resemblance.

The ovade wore a gold chain round his neck. And the apprentice when initiated has a silk cord, in masonic parlance a *cable-tow*, suspended from his throat. Like the ovade, the apprentice is blindfolded, and as the former was led through the mazes of a labyrinth, the latter is led backwards and forwards, and in various directions.

Thunder and lightning were counterfeited in the initiation of a Druid, and in that of the Royal Arch the Companions fire pistols, clash swords, overturn chairs, and roll cannon balls across the floor.

The tiler stands at the door with a drawn sword.

And tests of fortitude though less severe than in former times are not unknown among Masons. The following arduous trial was used in the Female Lodges of Paris :—

"A candidate for admission was usually very much excited. During a part of the ceremony she was conducted to an eminence, and told to look down at what awaited her if she faltered in her duty. Beneath her appeared a frightful abyss in which a double row of iron spikes were visible. No doubt her mind was in a chaos of fanaticism, for instead of shrinking at the sight, she exclaimed " I can encounter all," and sprang forward. At that moment a secret spring was touched, and the candidate fell not on the spikes, but on a green bed in imitation of a verdant plain. She fainted but was soon recovered by her friends, when the scene having changed she was reanimated and soothed by the sweet strains of choral music."

I have already shown, I trust conclusively, that the Druidic mysteries were founded on those of the Egyptians, and were analogous to those of Tyre, Persia and Hindostan; and that their moral doctrines and pristine simplicity of worship were those of the Hebrew Patriarchs.

It will be easy to show that those of Freemasonry, if not a mere perpetuation of the Druidic were derived from the same fountains, and that the secrets of this science and philosophy are hidden from us by the veil of Isis.

To the Egyptian candidate on his initiation, the Hierophant displayed the holy volume of hieroglyphics which he then restored to its repository.

So when the eyes of the apprentice are first released from darkness, he beholds the volume of the sacred law.

During the Persian initiations, the doctrine was enforced *ex cathedra*, from the desk or pulpit. So the Grand Master sits on a throne before which the candidate kneels, pointing a dagger to his naked left breast and two white wands being crossed above his head.

On the seal of the ancient Abbey of Arbroath in Scotland, is a representation which bears a curious

resemblance to the engraving on a seal used by the
priests of Isis, and which Plutarch describes in his
Essay on Isis and Osiris—*a man kneeling, his hands
bound, and a knife at his throat.*

In all the ancient mysteries before an aspirant
could claim participation in the higher secrets of
the institution, he was placed within the *pastos* or
bed, or *coffin*, and was subjected to a confinement in
darkness for a certain time.

This I have described to be practiced by the
Druids. In some of their labyrinths, discovered in
France, the remains of cells have been found, and
there was a dark cell of probation recently standing
near Maidstone, Kitt's Cotti House—from *Ked* (or
Ceridwen) the British Isis, and *cotti* an ark, or
chest.

So in the initiation of a Master Mason, the candidate is in some lodges buried in a coffin to represent
the death of the murdered Hiram Abiff.

The grand festival of Masonry is on Midsummer
Day, which was also the grand festival of the Druids.

The processional movements of the Masons as of
the Druids were mostly circular.

I have already instanced the symbol by which the
Jews expressed the word 'Jehovah.' This letter
jod was believed by them to denote the presence of
God, especially when conveyed in a circle

Masons also have a word which they are not allowed
to pronounce except in the presence of a full lodge,
and they pay peculiar reverence to a point within a
circle.

Some of the Druidic monuments are simple circles
with a stone standing in the midst, and the boss in
the centre of their circular shields had probably the
same signification.

The Masonic Lodge, like all Pagan temples, is
built due east and west.   Its form is an oblong
square which the ancients believed to be the shape
of the world.   In the west are two pillars surmounted
by globes.   The one on the left is called Boaz, and
is supposed to represent Osiris or the sun, the other
Jachin, the emblem of Isis or the moon.   The floor
is mosaic, and the walls are adorned with the various
symbols of the craft.

The cross is one of the chief emblems in Masonry
as it was in Druidism, and in all the Pagan religions.
The Taw $\coprod$ is a badge in Royal Arch Masonry,
and almost all the other varieties of the symbol
are used in Masonry.

The key and the cross-keys are also mosaic symbols.   They are supposed to be astronomical signs
of Anubis, or the Dog-Star.

An ear-of-corn is a prominent emblem in Masonry,
proving that the order did not confine their intellects

and their labors to the building of houses, but devoted themselves also to agriculture.

A sprig of acacia is one of the emblems revered by the Masons, and answers to the Egyptian lotus, to the myrtle of Eleusis, to the golden branch of Virgil and to the Druidic mistletoe. It is curious that *Houzza* which Mahomet esteemed an idol— Houzza so honored in the Arabian works of Ghatfân Koreisch, Kenanah and Salem should be simply the acacia. Thence was derived the word *huzza!* in our language, which was probably at first a religious exclamation like the *Evohe!* of the Bacchantes.

The doctrines of Masonry are the most beautiful that it is possible to conceive. They breathe the simplicity of the earliest ages animated by the love of a martyred God.

That word which the Puritans translated "charity," but which is really "love"—love is the key-stone of the Royal Arch upon which is supported the entire system of this mystic science.

In the lectures of the French Lodges the whole duty of a Mason is summed up in this one brief sentence: "*Aimez-vous les uns les autres, instruisez-vous, secourez-vous, voilà tout notre livre, toute notre loi, toute notre science.*"

"Love one another, teach one another, help one

another.   That is all our doctrine, all our science, all our law."

Ah! rail against us bigoted and ignorant men, slander us curious and jealous women if you will. Those who obey the precepts of their masters, and those who listen to the truths which they inculcate can readily forgive you.   It is impossible to be a good Mason without being a good man.

We have no narrow-minded prejudices; we do not debar from our society this sect or that sect; it is sufficient for us that a man worships God, no matter under what name or in what manner, and we admit him.   Christians, Jews, Mahometans, Buddhists are enrolled among us, and it is in the Mason's Lodge alone that they can kneel down together without feeling hatred, without professing contempt against their brother worshippers.

III.

IN RUSTIC FOLK-LORE.

IT is strange with what pertinacity the ignorant retain those customs which their fathers observed, and which they hold sacred without understanding either their origin or their purpose.

It is an attribute of human nature to hallow all that belongs to the past. It is impossible to look without admiration upon a venerable building which has lived through centuries, an immortal work of art; it is natural that we should also revere those customs which have descended to us by no written laws, by no kingly proclamations, but simply from lip to ear, from father to son.

Before I enter the homes of our peasants however, come with me to the mountains of Wales where we shall find the true descendants, not only of the ancient Britons but also of the Holy Druids themselves.

I mean the Bards, or harpers, who still continue to strike melodious notes in this land of music and metheglin, and who still convey to their hearers the precepts of their great ancestors.

The Bards were always held in high reverence in Wales, and that is why they have lived so long. When the priests had been swept away by the sword of the new religion, this glorious association of musicians remained, and consented to sing praises to Jesus Christ the Redeemer, instead of to HU the pervading spirit.

Indeed it was said of Barach, who was chief Bard to Conchobhar Nessan, King of Ulster, that he described the passion of Jesus in such moving words that the king, transported with rage, drew his sword and fell to hacking and hewing the trees of the wood in which he was standing, mistaking them for Jews, and even died of the frenzy.

By studying the old Welsh laws of Howel the good king (A. D. 940), one finds some curious matter respecting the position which the Bards held at that time in the Court and country.

Y Bardd Teulu, or Court Bard (an appointment from which that of our poet-laureate probably originated) on receiving his commission, was presented by the king with a silver harp, by the queen with a gold ring. He held the eighth place at Court. He possessed his land free. At the three great festivals of the year, Christmas, Easter, and Whitsuntide, he sat at the prince's table. On these occasions, he was entitled to have the *disdain's* or steward-of-the-household's garment for his fee. In addition to these perquisites, the king found him in woolen robes, and the queen in linen, and he received a present from every maiden when she married, but nothing at the bridal feasts of women who had been married before.

At regal feasts the guests were placed in threes; a tune called *Gosteg yr Halen*, "the prelude of the salt," was sung as the salt-cellar was placed before the king, and as they were served with meats, &c., upon platters of clean grass and rushes, the harp played all the while.

When a song was called for after the feast, the *Oadeir-fardd*, or the bard who possessed the badge of-the-chair sang a hymn to the glory of God, and then another in honor of the king. After which, the *Teuluwr*, or Bard of the Hall sang upon some other subject.

If the queen wished for a song after she had retired to her apartment, the *Teuluwr*, might sing to her, but in a low voice, lest he disturb the other performers in the hall.

If a Bard desired a favor of the king, he was obliged to play one of his own compositions; if of a nobleman, three; and if of a villain, till he was exhausted.

His person was held so sacred that whoever slightly injured him was fined VI cows and CXX pence, and the murderer of a Bard was fined CXXVI cows. The worst murder in those days, like criminal conversations in the present age, only needed pecuniary atonement

On a plundering expedition, the Bard received a large portion of the spoil. He preceded the warriors to battle, reciting a poem called *Unbenaeth Prydain*, "the glory of Britain."

An edict was issued by King Edward I. authorizing the massacre of the Bards, one of them having prophesied the liberation of Wales. The murder of the last Bard has been beautifully described by Gray in one of his poems.

Queen Elizabeth also issued a proclamation, but of a less sanguinary character against certain wandering minstrels, who appear to have been among the musicians of those days what quacks are among our modern M. D.'s. It also commissioned certain gentlemen to inquire into the various capabilities of the Welsh Bards, and to license those who were most fit to represent the musical talent of their country.

This profound question was settled at an *Eisteddfod*, or a musical meeting of the Bard who contested once a year for a silver harp. This practice which had existed from time immemorial is still continued in Wales, and the transactions of the *Aberffraw Royal Eisteddfod* were published in the year 1849.

I know little of the peculiar character of Welsh music except that it is executed mostly in B flat. Part-singing may be considered as a peculiarity of the Welsh bards. Extempore performances were common to all the ancient minstrels of the world.

A kind of extempore composition is still exercised among the Welsh peasantry, and is called *Penillion* singing. The harper being seated, plays one of his native airs while the singers stand round him and alternately compose a stanza upon any subject they please.

There are many *clerwyr*, or wandering minstrels still in Wales. Like their predecessors, they are in the habit of going from house to house, and of officiating, as our gypsy fiddlers do at all rustic festivals and weddings.

They have a curious tradition, that Madoc, a brother of one of the Kings of Wales, sailed from that country in the year 1171 A. D. and was the first European settler in Mexico. Sir Thomas Herbert who wrote a scarce book of travels in 1665, mentions it as a fact, and in Hackett's Collection of Epitaphs (1757) is this one:—

FOUND AT MEXICO.

"Madoc wyf mwydic ei wedd
Iawn genau Owain Gwynedd
Ni fynnwn dir fy awydd oedd
Na da mawr ond y Moroedd."

"Madoc I am—mild in countenance
Of the right line of Owen Gwynedd
I wished not for land ; my bent was
For no great riches, but for the seas.

We have it on the authority of a Captain **Davies,** and Lieutenant Roberts of Hawcorden in Flintshire, and from a MS. entry in William Penn's journal, evidence collected by the famous Dr. Owen Pughe, that the tribes of the Illinois, Madocautes, the Padoucas and Mud Indians spoke the Welsh language.

Without entering into a useless dissertation upon this subject, I will note a curious custom in which the American Indians resemble the Welsh, viz., in the habit of carrying their canoes upon their backs from rapid to rapid. Giraldus Cambrensis informs us that the Welsh used to carry their triangular boats from river to river, which occasioned a famous dealer, named Bledherc, to say: "There is amongst us a people who when they go out in search of prey carry their horses on their backs to the place of plunder; in order to catch their prey, they leap upon their horses, and when it is taken, carry their horses home again upon their shoulders."

They worshipped the same symbols of God as the

ancient British—the sun, the moon, fire, water, the serpent, the cross, &c., and in the course of this chapter I shall mention other customs common to both nations.

. . . .

Among the peasantry of Great Britain and Ireland, there are observed not only those traditional customs which are meaningless because they are out of date, but actual idolatries.

It may surprise the reader that the worship of fire with which our preachers and tract-writers jeer the inhabitants of Persia, is not yet extinct among us.

Spenser says that the Irish never lighted a fire without uttering a prayer. In some parts of England it is considered unlucky for the fire to go out. They have a peculiar fuel with which they feed it during the night. The Scotch peat-fires are seldom allowed to die out.

There are three days in the year on which the worship of fire is especially observed—May-day, Midsummer Eve and Allhallow E'en.

On the first of May which is called *Beltan*, or *Beltein*-Day from the Druidic *Beltenus*, the Phœnician *Baal*, the Highland herdsmen assemble on a moor. They cut a table in the sod, of a round figure, by casting a trench in the ground of such circumference as to hold the whole company. They kindle a wood fire and dress a large caudle of eggs, butter, oatmeal and milk, taking care to be supplied with plenty of beer and whiskey as well. The rites begin with spilling some of the caudle on the ground by way of a libation; on that, every one takes a cake of oatmeal, upon which are raised nine square knobs, each dedicated to some particular being, the supposed preserver of their flocks and herbs, or to some particular animal the real destroyer of them. Each person then turns his face to the fire, breaks off a knob and flinging it over his shoulder, says: *This I give to thee, preserve thou my horses; this I give to thee, preserve thou my sheep,* and so on. After that, they use the same ceremony to the noxious animals. *This I give to thee, oh fox! spare thou my lambs! this to thee, oh hooded crow; this to thee, oh eagle!*

They then knead another cake of oatmeal which is toasted at the embers against a stone. They divide this cake into so many portions (as similar as possible to each other in size and shape) as there are persons in the company. They daub one of these portions all over with charcoal until it is quite black. They put all the bits into a bonnet and every one, blind-folded, draws. He who holds the bonnet is entitled to the last bit. Whoever draws the black morsel is the devoted person who is to be sacrificed to Baal, and is compelled to leap three times through the fire, after which they dine on the caudle.

When the feast is finished, the remains are concealed by two persons deputed for that purpose, and on the next Sunday they re-assemble and finish it.

This, you see, is a relic of the Druidic human sacrifices as well as of their fire-worship. I will give two more examples of the former.

I have noticed the custom of the Druids in great extremities of constructing a large wicker engine, of filling it with sheep, oxen and sometimes men, and setting light to it, as a mammoth sacrifice. Dr. Milner in his History of Winchester, informs us that at Dunkirk and at Douay there has existed an immemorial custom of constructing huge figures of wicker-work and canvas, and moving them about to represent a giant that was killed by their patron saint. And St. Foix, in his Essay on Paris, describes a custom which is not yet abolished in some of the small towns in France, viz., for the mayors on the Eve of St. John to put into a large basket a dozen or two cats, and to throw them into one of the festive bonfires lighted upon that occasion.

To return to May Day. In Munster and Connaught the Irish peasants drive their cattle between two fires, as if for purposes of purification. In some parts of Scotland they light a fire to feast by, and having thrown a portion of their refreshments into the flames as a propitiatory sacrifice, deck branches of mountain-ash with wreaths of flowers and heather, and walk three times round it in a procession.

Precisely the same custom is observed by the natives of America and at the same period, *i. e.*, that of the vernal equinox.

In India there is a festival in honor of *Bhavani* (a Priapic personification of nature and fecundity), which the Hindoos commemorate by erecting a pole in the fields, and by adorning it with pendants and flowers round which the young people dance precisely the same as in England.

The Jews also keep a solar festival at the vernal equinox, on which occasion the Paschal lamb is sacrificed.

The Floridians and Mexicans erect a tree in the centre of their sacred enclosures around which they dance.

On May Eve the Cornish erect stumps of trees before their doors. On the first of the month the famous May-pole is raised, adorned with flowers and encircled by the pretty country lasses who little know of what this pole, or φαλλος is an emblem.

On Midsummer Eve an involuntary tribute is paid by the peasants of Great Britain and Ireland to the shades of their ancient priests, and to the Gods whom they worshipped, by lighting bonfires. The word bonfire, I may observe, is by some called *bone-fire* because they believe (without any particular reason), that their fuel consisted of bones; by others *boon-fire*, because the wood was obtained by begging. *Utrum horum marvis accipe.*

The cooks of Newcastle lighted fires on Midsummer Day in the streets of that town; the custom is general almost all over Ireland, and as late as the year 1786, the custom of lighting fires was continued in the Druidic Temple at Bramham, near Harrowgate in Yorkshire, on the eve of the summer solstice.

In the Cornish tongue, Midsummer is called *Goluan*, which means light and rejoicing. At that season, the natives make a procession through the towns or villages with lighted torches.

The Irish dance round these fires, and sometimes fathers, taking their children in their arms, will run through the flames.

In Hindostan it is the mother who performs this office

On all sacred days among the Druids, they resorted to their different kinds of divination, and I should tire the reader were I to enumerate half the charms and incantations which are made use of in the country on Midsummer Eve.

I have always remarked that those divinations

which were probably used by priests to foretell the
fate of a kingdom, or to decide upon the life or death
of a human being, have now become mere methods
of love prophecies with village sweethearts.

One will sow hemp-seed on Midsummer Eve,
saying, *Hemp-seed I sow, hemp-seed I hoe, and he that
is my true love come after me and mow.* She will then
turn round, and expects to see the young man who
will marry her.

Another will pick a kind of root which grows
under mug-wort, and which, if pulled exactly at
midnight on the Eve of St. John the Baptist and
placed under her pillow, will give her a dream of her
future husband.

Another will place over her head the orphine-
plant, commonly called *Midsummer-men:* the bend-
ing of the leaves to the right or to the left will tell
her whether her husband was true or false.

Bourne cites from the Trullan Council a species
of divination, so singular, that it is impossible to
read it without being reminded of the Pythoness on
her tripod, or the Druidess on her seat of stone.

"On the 23rd of June, which is the Eve of St.
John the Baptist, men and women were accustomed
to gather together in the evening at the sea-side or
in certain houses, and there adorn a girl who was
her father's first-begotten child after the manner of

a bride. Then they feasted and leaped after the
manner of Bacchanals, and danced and shouted as
they were wont to do on their holy-days; after this,
they poured into a narrow-necked vessel some of
the sea-water, and also put into it certain things
belonging to each of them. Then as if the devil
gifted the girl with the faculty of telling future things,
they would enquire with a loud voice about the
good or evil fortune that should attend them; upon
this the girl took out of the vessel the first thing
that came to hand and showed it, and gave it to the
owner, who, upon receiving it, was so foolish as to
imagine himself wiser, as to the good or evil fortune
that should attend him."

The Druidic vervain was held in estimation on this
day as we read in *Ye Popish Kingdome.*

Then doth ye joyful feast of John ye Baptist take his turne,
When bonfiers great with lofty flame in every town doe burne,
And young men round about with maides doe dance in every streete,
With garlands wrought of mother-wort, or else with verwain sweete.

The following extract from the Calendar of the
Romish Church, shows us what doings there used to
be at Rome on the Eve and Day of St. John the
Baptist—the Roman Pales—the Druidic Belenus.

JUNE.

23.   The Virgil of the Nativity of John the Baptist.
       Spices are given at Vespers.
       Fires are lighted up.
       A girl with a little drum that proclaims the garland.
       Boys are dressed in girl's clothes:

Carols to the liberal: imprecations against the avaricious.
Waters are swum in during the night, and are brought in vessels
that hang for purposes of divination.
Fern in great estimation with the vulgar on account of its seed.
Herbs of different kinds are sought with many ceremonies.
Girl's Thistle is gathered, and a hundred crosses by the same.
24. The Nativity of John the Baptist.
Dew and new leaves in estimation.
The vulgar solstice.

It was on Hallow–E'en that the Druids used to
compel their subjects to extinguish their fires, which,
when the annual dues were paid, were relighted
from that holy fire which burnt in the *clachan* of the
Druids, and which never died.

Even now all fires are extinguished on Hallow-
E'en, and a fire being made by rubbing two sticks
together they are relighted from that, and from that
alone.

The same custom is observed among the Cherokee
Indians.

At the village of Findern in Derbyshire, the boys
and girls go every year on the 2nd of November
and light a number of small fires among the furze
growing there, which they call *Tindles*. They can
give no reason for so doing.

Throughout the United Kingdom there are similar
divining customs observed to those which I have
just described as exercised on Midsummer Eve.

There are miscellaneous vestiges of fire–worship
besides those already noticed.

In Oxfordshire revels, young women will sometimes tuck their skirts (twisting them in an ingenious
manner round the ankles, and holding the ends in
front of them) into a very good resemblance of
men's trousers, and dance round a candle placed
upon the floor, concluding by leaping over it three
times. The name of this dance, too coarse to be
written here, as the dance is to be described, betrays
its phallic origin.

Then there is the "*Dance round our coal fire,*"
an ancient practice of dancing round the fires in the
Inns of Court, which was observed in 1733, at an
entertainment at the Inner Temple Hall on Lord
Chancellor Talbot's taking leave of the house, when
"the Master of the Revels took the Chancellor by
the hand, and he Mr. Page, who with the Judges,
Sergeants and Benchers danced round the Coal
Fire, according to the old ceremony three times;
and all the time the ancient song with music was
sung by a man in a bar gown."

Last and most singular of all the *Tinegin*, or need-
fire of the Highlanders.

To defeat sorceries, certain persons appointed to
do so are sent to raise the need-fire. By any small
river or lake, or upon any island a circular booth of
turf or stone is erected, on which a rafter of birch-
tree is placed and the roof covered over. In the

centre is set a perpendicular post, fixed by a wooden pin to the couple, the lower end being placed in an oblong groove on the floor, and another pole placed horizontally between the upright post and the leg of the couple into both of which the ends being tapered are inserted. This horizontal timber is called the auger, being provided with four short spokes by which it can be turned. As many men as can be collected are then set to work. Having divested themselves of all kinds of metals, they turn the pole two at a time by means of the levers, while others keep driving wedges under the upright post so as to press it against the auger, which by the friction soon becomes ignited. From this the need-fire is instantly procured, and all other fires being quenched, those that are rekindled both in dwelling houses and offices are accounted sacred, and the diseased and bewitched cattle are successively made to smell them.

This contrivance is elaborate and its description not unnaturally awkward. It is however worthy of remark that in the initiation of Freemasons all metals are taken from them.

. . . .

Water was worshipped by the Druids, and was used by them for purification. The Welsh peasantry hold sacred the rain-water which lodges in the crevices of their cromleachs or altars, and the Irish proverb " To take a dip in the Shannon," would seem to show that its waters were held in the same superstitious reverence as are those of the Ganges by the natives of Hindostan.

The Druids besprinkled themselves with dew when they went to sacrifice, and it is a belief among the English lasses that those who bathe their faces in the dew on May Day morning will have beautiful complexions.

It is a belief in Oxfordshire that to cure a man bitten by a mad dog, he should be taken to the sea and dipped therein nine times.

The regard still paid, however, to wells and fountains by the peasantry is the most extraordinary feature of water-worship. In the early ages it prevailed with such strength, that the Roman Catholics fearing to combat the custom christianized it by giving the holy wells the names of popular saints, and by enjoining pilgrimages after the Pagan fashion to their shrine.

In some parts of England it is still customary to decorate these wells with boughs of trees, garlands of tulips, and other flowers placed in various fancied devices.

At one time, indeed it was the custom on Holy Thursday, after the service for the day at the church, for the clergyman and singers to pray and sing psalms at these wells.

Pilgrimages are still made by invalids among the poor Irish to wells, whose waters are supposed to possess medicinal properties under the influence of some beneficent saint.

The well of Strathfillan in Scotland is also resorted to at certain periods of the year. The water of the well of Trinity Gask in Perthshire is supposed to cure any one seized with the plague. In many parts of Wales the water used for the baptismal font is fetched from these holy wells.

Not only a reverence, but actual sacrifices are offered to some of these wells and to the saints which preside over them, or to the spirits which are supposed to inhabit them.

In a quillet, called *Gwern Degla*, near the village of Llandegla in Wales there is a small spring. The water is under the tutelage of St. Tecla and is esteemed a sovereign remedy for the falling sickness. The patient washes his limbs in the well, makes an offering into it of fourpence, walks round it three times, and thrice repeats the Lord's prayer. If a man, he sacrifices a cock; if a woman a hen. The fowl is carried in a basket first round the well, after that into the churchyard and round the church. The votary then enters the church, gets under the communion table, lies down with the Bible under his head, is covered with a cloth and rests there till break of day. When he departs, he offers sixpence and leaves the fowl in the church. If the bird dies, the cure is supposed to have been affected and the disease transferred to the devoted victim.

The custom of sticking bits of rag on thorns near these wells is inexplicable, as it is universal. Between the walls of Alten and Newton, near the foot of Rosberrye Toppinge, there is a well dedicated to St. Oswald. The neighbors have a belief that a shirt or shift taken off a sick person and thrown into the well will prognosticate his fate. If it floats the person will recover, if it sinks he will die. And to reward the saint for his intelligence, they tear a rag off the shirt and leave it hanging on the briars thereabouts, "*where*" says Grose, citing a MS. in the Cotton Library, marked Julius F. vi. "*I have seen such numbers as might have made a fayre rheme in a papermyll.*"

That the Highlanders still believe in spirits which inhabit their lakes is easily proved. In Strathspey there is a lake called *Loch nan Spiordan*, the Lake of Spirits. When its waters are agitated by the wind and its spray mounts whirling in the air, they believe that it is the anger of this spirit whom they name *Martach Shine*, or the Rider of the Storm.

The Well of St. Keyne in the parish of St. Keyne, in Cornwall, is supposed to possess a curious property which is humorously explained in the following verses :—

THE WELL OF ST. KEYNE.

A well there is in the west country,
And a clearer one never was seen—
There is not a wife in the west country
But has heard of the Well of St. Keyne.

An oak and an elm tree stand beside,
And behind doth an ash tree grow,
And a willow from the bank above
Droops to the water below.

A traveler came to the Well of St. Keyne,
Pleasant it was to his eye ;
For from cock-crow he had been traveling,
And there was not a cloud in the sky.

He drank of the water so cool and clear,
For thirsty and hot was he ;
And he sat him down upon the bank,
Under the willow tree.

There came a man from a neighboring town,
At the well to fill his pail;
On the well-side he rested it,
And bade the stranger hail.

Now, art thou a bachelor, stranger? quoth he,
For an if thou hast a wife,
The happiest draught thou hast drank this day
That ever thou didst in thy life.

Or has your good woman, if one you have,
    In Cornwall ever been ?
For an if she have, I'll venture my life,
She has drunk of the Well of St. Keyne.

I have left a good woman who never was here,
The stranger he made reply;
But that my draught should be better for that,
I pray thee tell me why.

St. Keyne, quoth the countryman, many a time,
Drank of this chrystal well;
And before the angel summoned her,
She laid on the water a spell.

If the husband, (of this gifted well),
Shall drink before his wife,
A happy man thenceforth is he,
For he shall be master for life.

But if the wife should drink of it first,
God help the husband then !
The stranger stooped to the well of St. Keyne,
And drank of its waters again.

You drank of the well I warrant betimes?
He to the countryman said,
But the countryman smiled as the stranger spoke,
And sheepishly shook his head.

I hastened as soon as the wedding was done.
And left my wife in the porch,
But i'faith I found her wiser than me,
For she took a bottle to church.

I must not omit to mention a method of divination
by water, which is practiced at Madern Well in the
parish of Madern, and at the well of St. Ennys, in
the parish of Sancred, Cornwall. At a certain period
of the year, moon or day, come the uneasy, impatient
and superstitious, and by dropping pins or pebbles
into the water, and by shaking the ground round the
spring so as to raise bubbles from the bottom, endeavor to predict the future. This practice is not
indigenous to Britain. The Castalian fountain in
Greece was supposed to be of a prophetic nature.
By dipping a mirror into a well the Patræans received,
as they supposed, omens of ensuing sickness or

health from the figures portrayed upon its surface. In Laconia, they cast into a lake, sacred to Juno, three stones, and drew prognostications from the several turns which they made in sinking.

I will translate at length a pretty French story which I have met with, and which will adorn as well as illustrate the present subject.

THE LEGEND OF THE PIN.

In the West of France the pin is endowed with a fabulous power, which is not without a certain interest. One of its supposed attributes is the power of attracting lovers to her who possess it, after it has been used in the toilet of a bride. Consequently it is a curious sight in La Vendeé or Les Deux-Sèvres, to see all the peasant girls anxiously placing a pin in the bride's dress: the number being often so considerable that she is forced to have a pin-cushion attached to her waist-band to receive all the prickly charms. At night, on the threshold of the bridal chamber, she is surrounded by her companions, each one easily seizing upon the charmed pin, which is kept as a sacred relic.

In Brittany the pin is regarded as the guardian of chastity, a mute witness which will one day stand forth to applaud or condemn in the following manner :—

Some days before the wedding, the betrothed leads his future bride to the edge of some mysterious current of water, and taking one of her pins drops it into the water. If it swims, the girl's innocence is incontestable—if on the contrary it sinks to the bottom, it is considered the judgment of heaven; it is an accusation which no evidence can overcome. But as the peasant girls in Brittany never use any pins heavier than the long blackthorn, which they find in the hedges, the severity of the tribunal is not very formidable.

On the 7th of December, a young peasant mounted on a strong cob, full of hope and gaiety, was seen urging his way towards Morlaix with a handsome girl of twenty on a pillion behind him, her arm tenderly clasping his waist. It was easy to see in their happy faces that they were two lovers, and from the direction which they took, that they were going on a pilgrimage to try the charm of the pin at the fountain of St. Douet. Jean's father was one of the richest land-holders in the neighborhood, but above all the young ladies round him, he had chosen Margaret, whose sole wealth consisted in her beauty and virtue.

Through all the glades of the wood with wild thyme and violets beneath their horses feet, they journeyed on till they came to a wild and deserted plain, whence they plunged once more into the dark forests of Finisterre filled with Druidical memories. It might have been those sombre shades which saddened them for a moment, but it was only for a moment. Jean feared not the trial, for he loved Margaret, and believed her to be an angel. And Margaret feared it not, for she knew that she was innocent.

Now they were close to the sacred fountain, which burst through the crevices of a rock overgrown with moss into a natural bason, and thence like a thread of silver through the forest.

They dismounted, and Margaret, kneeling down, prayed fervently for some moments. Then rising, she gave her left hand to her lover, and full of confidence, advanced toward the well. Alas! she had too much faith in the virtue of the legend. Instead of a thorn pin, she took from a neckerchief one with a silver head which he had given her. He pressed her fingers affectionately as he took it from her hand and dropped it into the well. It disappeared instantaneously. Margaret sank to the ground with a heart-broken groan.

He raised her and placed her on his horse, but he did not speak to her, he did not caress her. In mournful silence he walked by her side. Her arm could no longer embrace him. She was not his

Margaret now. She was a guilty wretch who had dared to tempt the judgment of God.

He placed her down at her father's door, and stooping he kissed her on the forehead. It was a silent adieu he was bidding her; it was his last kiss —it was the kiss of death.

Next morning her corpse was found underneath his window. There were no marks of violence upon her body; the wound was in her heart; she had died a victim to a destestable superstition.

   .   .   .   .

To the element of air we do not find our peasants pay any particular homage, unless the well-known practice of sailors of whistling for the wind in a dead calm, and of the Cornish laborers when engaged in winnowing may be regarded as such.

But the worship of the heavenly bodies has not yet died out among us. The astrologists of the middle ages were but copyists of the ancient Chaldeans, and the lower classes to this day draw omens from meteors and falling stars. General Vallancey, by the way, records a curious instance in his *Collectanea de rebus Hibernicis*, of an Irish peasant who could neither read nor write but who could calculate eclipses.

When we consider how universal and how prominent was the worship of the sun in the world, it is almost surprising that we do not find more vestiges of this idolatry. There are some few however.

It was once a custom of the vulgar to rise early on Easter Day to see the sun dance, for they fancied that the reflection of its beams played or danced upon the waters of any spring or lake they might look into.

In the British Apollo, fol. Lond. 1708, vol. i. No. 40, we read:

> Q. Old wives, Phœbus, say
>   That on Easter day,
>   To the music o' the spheres you do caper,
>   If the fact, sir, be true,
>   Pray let's the cause know,
>   When you have any room in your paper.
>
> A. The old wives get merry,
>   With spic'd ale or sherry,
>   On Easter, which makes them romance
>   And whilst in a rout,
>   Their brains whirl about,
>   They fancy we caper and dance.

The sun shining on the bride as she goes to church is a good omen. The cloudy rising of the sun is a presage of misfortune. The Highlanders, when they approach a well to drink, walk round it from east to west, sometimes thrice.

The Orkney fishermen, on going to sea, would think themselves in imminent peril, were they by accident to turn their boat in opposition to the sun's course; and I have seen many well-educated people seriously discomfited if the cards from the pack, the balls from the pool-basket, or the decanters at the dining-table had not been sent round *as the sun goes*.

All the ancient dances were in imitation of the revolutions of the heavenly bodies, and were used in religious worship. Such were the circular dances of the Druids—the slower and statelier movements of the Greek strophe—the dances of the Cabiri or Phœnician priests, the devotional dances of the Turkish dervishes, the Hindoo *Raas Jattra* or dance-of-the-circle, and the war dances of the American and other savage nations round their camp-fires, lodges, or triumphal poles.

Such also is the Round About, or Cheshire Round, which is referred to by Goldsmith in his Vicar of Wakefield, and which is not yet extinct in England.

But the best instance of sun-worship is found in the fires lighted by the common Irish on Midsummer's Eve, and which they tell you candidly are burnt "*in honor of the sun*."

The fires which the Scotch Highlanders light on May Day are to welcome back the sun after his long pilgrimage in the frosts and darkness of winter.

Crantz in his History of Greenland, informs us that the natives of that country observe a similar festival to testify their joy at the re-appearance of the sun, and the consequent renewal of the hunting season.

In matters of divination, the moon is supposed by the vulgar to possess a peculiar power. She was supposed to exercise an influence not only over the tides of the sea, and over the minds of men, but also over the future, in weather, cookery, and physic.

When the moon is encircled by a halo, or is involved in a mist, when she is called "greasy," it portends rain—when she is sharp horned, windy weather. It is also a general belief among all classes that as the weather is at the new moon, so it will continue during the whole month.

In many of the old almanacs and books of husbandry, it is directed to kill hogs when the moon is increasing, and the bacon will prove the better, in boiling; to shear sheep at the moon's increase; to fell hand-timber from the full to the change; to fell frith, coppice, and fuel at the first quarter; to geld cattle when the moon is in Aries, Sagittarius, or Capricorn.

In *The Husbandman's Practice*, or *Prognostication for ever*, the reader is advised "To purge with electuaries the moon in Cancer, with pills the moone in Pisces, with potions the moone in Virgo," and in another place, "To set, sow seeds, graft, and plant, the moone being in Taurus, Virgo or Capricorn, and all kinds of corne in Cancer, to graft in March, at the moone's increase, she being in Taurus or Capricorn."

Werenfels in his Dissertation on Superstition, speaking of a superstitious man, writes, " He will have his hair cut either when the moon is in Leo, that his locks may stare like the lion's shag, or in Aries that they may stare like a ram's horn. Whatever he would have to grow he sets about when she is in the increase; for whatever he would have made less he chooses her wane. When the moon is in Taurus, he can never be persuaded to take physic, lest that animal which chews its cud should make him cast it up again; and if at any time he has a mind to be admitted to the presence of a prince, he will wait till the moon is in conjunction with the sun, for 'tis then the society of an inferior with a superior is salutary and successful."

The islanders of Sky will not dig peats (which is their only fuel) in the increase of the moon, believing that they are less moist, and will burn more clearly if cut in the wane.

In the parishes of Kirkwall and St. Ola, Orkney, none marry or kill cattle in the wane.

In Angus it is believed that if a child be put from the breast during the waning of the moon, it will

decay all the time that the moon continues to wane.
I will mention two more instances of divination,
one from Thomas Hodge's *Incarnate Divells*, viz.,
"That when the moone appeareth in the spring-
time, the one horn spotted and hidden with a blacke
and great cloude from the first day of her apparition
to the fourth day after, it is some signe of tempests
and troubles in the aire the summer after."

When the new moon appears with the old moon
in her arms, or in other words when that part of the
moon which is covered by the shadow of the earth
is seen through it, it is considered not only an omen
of bad weather, but also of misfortune, as we learn
from the following stanza in the ballad of *Sir Patrick
Spence* :

> Late, late yestreen I saw the new moone
> Wi' the auld moone in her arme;
> And I feir, I feir, my deir master,
> That we will come to harm.

One might enumerate examples of this kind to
volumes, and I fear I have already passed the limits
of human endurance; I must, however, write a few
words upon the subject of moon-worship.

The feminine appellation is traditionally derived
from the fable of Isis, who was entitled the wife of
the sun. The superstition of the man-in-the-moon,
is supposed to have originated in the account given
in the Book of Numbers, XV. 32 *et seq.* of a man

punished with death for gathering sticks on the Sabbath Day, though why, it is difficult to explain. In Ritson's Ancient Songs we read, " The man-in-the-moon is represented leaning upon a fork, on which he carries a bush of thorn, because it was for ' pycchynde stake' on a Sunday that he is reported to have been thus confined." And in Midsummer Night's Dream, one of the actors says, " All I have to say is to tell you that the lantern is the moon, I the man-in-the-moon, this thorn bush my thorn bush, and this dog my dog." *Vide* also Tempest, act. ii. sc. 2.

The new moon still continues to be idolatrously worshipped by the vulgar of many countries.

On the night of the new moon, the Jews assemble to pray to God under the names of the Creator of the planets, and the restorer of the moon.

The Madingoe Tribe of African Indians whisper a short prayer with their hands held before their face; they then spit upon their hands and religiously anoint their faces with the same.

At the end of the Mahometan Feast of Rhamadan (which closely resembles the Romish Carnival) the priests await the reappearance of the moon, and salute her with clapping of hands, beating of drums and firing of muskets.

In the 65th Canon of the 6th council of Constantinople, A. D. 680, is the following interdiction: "Those bone-fires that are kindled by certaine people on new moones before their shops and houses, over which also they are most foolishly and ridiculously to leape by a certaine antient custom, we command them from henceforth to cease. Whoever therefore shall do any such thing, if he be a clergyman let him be deposed—if a layman let him be excommunicated."

No bonfires are now lit in honor of the new moon, but the common Irish on beholding her for the first time cross themselves, saying:

"May thou leave us as safe as thou hast found us."

English peasants often salute the new moon, saying: "There is the new moon, God bless her," usually seating themselves on a stile as they do so.

They also believe that a new moon seen over the right shoulder is lucky, over the left shoulder unlucky, and straight before good luck to the end of the moon.

That if they look straight at the new moon (or a shooting star) when they first see it, and wish for something, their wish will be fulfilled before the end of the year.

The peasant girls, in some parts of England, when they see the new moon in the new year, take their stocking off from one foot and run to the next stile; when they get there, they look between the great toe and the next, and expect to find a hair which will be the color of their lover's.

In Yorkshire, it is common enough for an inquisitive maid to go out into a field till she finds a stone fast in the earth, to kneel upon this with naked knees and looking up at the new moon to say:

> All hail, new moon, all hail to thee,
> I prithee, good moon, reveal to me
> This night, who shall my true love be,
> Who he is, and what he wears,
> And what he does all months and years.

She then retires *backwards* till she comes to a stile, and goes to bed directly without speaking a word.

The Irish believe that eclipses of the moon are effected by witchcraft, and this occasions me to narrate a curious custom of the ancient Peruvians who were the Egyptians of the New World.

When the moon became eclipsed, they imagined that she was ill and would fall down and crush the world. Accordingly as soon as the eclipse commenced, they made a noise with cornets and drums, and tying dogs to trees beat them till they howled in order to awake the fainting moon who is said to love these animals, for Diana and Nehalenna are seldom represented without a dog by their side.

Since we find in a book, called Osborne's Advice to his Son, p. 79, that "the Irish and Welch during eclipses ran about beating kettles and pans, thinking their clamor and vexations available to the assistance of the higher orbes," it is probable that they made use of the same canine resources as the natives of Peru, and that such is the origin of the Irish proverb that "*dogs will bark at the moon.*"

.   .   .   .

Having thus considered the worship of the elements and of the heavenly bodies extant among us, let us pass on to those minor idolatries which are still retained among the lower orders.

There is no religious custom of the Russians so celebrated as that of presenting each other with eggs dyed and stained, saying, "Christ is risen." To which the other replies "He is indeed," and they exchange kisses.

An egg was the Egyptian emblem of the universe, and it was from the Egyptians that all the Pagan nations, and afterwards the Greek Christians derived this ceremony. They are used also by the Roman Catholics and by the Jews in their Paschal festival.

It is probable that it was also a Druidic ceremony, for it prevails in Cumberland and many other counties of England. On Easter Monday and Tuesday the inhabitants assemble in the meadows, the children provided with hard boiled eggs, colored or ornamented in various ways, some being dyed with logwood or cochineal; others tinged with the juice of herbs and broom-flowers; others stained by being boiled in shreds of parti-colored riband; and others covered with gilding. They roll them along the ground, or toss them in the air till they break when they eat them—a part of the ceremony which they probably understand the best. They are called *pace-eggs* or *paste-eggs*, probably corrupted from *pasche*.

This reminds us of the strange fable of the serpent's egg. As I mentioned in an earlier chapter many of these eggs or adder-stones are preserved with great reverence in the Highlands. There are also some traditions upon this subject which are worth narrating.

Monsieur Chorier in his *Histoire de Dauphiné* informs us that in the divers parts of that county, especially near the mountain of Rochelle on the borders of Savoy, serpents congregate from the 15th of June to the 15th of August for purposes of generation. The place which they have occupied after they have gone, is covered with a sticky white foam which is indescribably disgusting to behold.

Camden relates that in most parts of Wales and throughout Scotland and Cornwall, it is an opinion of the vulgar that about Midsummer Eve the snakes meet together in companies, and that by joining heads together and hissing, a kind of bubble is formed which the rest by continual hissing blow on till it quite passes through the body, when it immediately hardens and resembles a glass ring which will make its finder prosperous in all his undertakings. The rings thus generated are called *gleinu madroeth*, or snake stones. They are small glass amulets commonly about half as wide as our finger rings, but much thicker, of a green color usually though sometimes blue and waved with red and white.

Careu in his *Survey of Cornwall* says that its inhabitants believe that snakes breathing upon a hazel wand produce a stone ring of a blue color, in which there appears the yellow figure of a snake, and that beasts which have been bit by a mad dog or poisoned, if given some water to drink wherein this stone has been infused, will perfectly recover.

The following custom is evidently a dramatic representation of the rape of the serpent's egg à la Pliny:

On Easter Monday, in Normandy, the common people congregate *à la motte de Pougard* which they surround. They place at the foot a basket containing a hundred eggs, the number of the stones of the temple of Aubury. A man takes the eggs and places them singly on the top of the tumulus, and then descends in the same manner to return them to the basket. While this is doing, another man runs to a village half a league off, and if he can return before the last egg is restored to the basket, he gains a barrel of cider as a prize, which he empties with the co-operation of his friends, and a Bacchanalian dance round the tumulus ends the proceedings.

Serpent-worship is almost extinct, if not entirely so; and the belief of the lower orders in Ireland that St. Patrick expelled all the snakes and other reptiles from the island is perhaps derived from his having extinguished their adorers.

However, it is considered unlucky in England to kill the harmless green snake; and there is a superstition almost universally present, that it will not die till the setting of that sun, of which it was an emblem.

Its tenacity of life is indeed something marvelous. Mr. Payne Knight, in his work on Phallic worship, (which I read at the British Museum, but which is somewhat absurdly excluded from the catalogue) states that he has seen the heart of an adder throb for some moments after it had been completely taken from the body, and even renew its beatings ten minutes afterwards when dipped in hot water.

Many of our ladies wear bracelets in the shape of a snake, as did the Egyptian dames of old. The lower orders believe that a serpent's skin will extract thorns, and its fat is sold to London chemists at five shillings a pound for its medicinal properties.

Most curious of all, is the superstition that by eating snakes one may grow young, and of which the three following passages are illustrations.

"A gentlewoman told an ancient bachelor, who looked very young, that she thought he had eaten a snake. No mistress, (he said) it is because I never meddled with any snakes which maketh me look so young."—*Holy State*, 1642, p. 36.

He hath left off o' late to feed on snakes,
His beard's turned white again.
Massinger, Old Law. Act V. Sc. I.

He is your loving brother, sir, and will tell nobody
But all he meets, that you have eat a snake,
And are grown young, gamesome, and rampant.
Ibid, Elder Brother, Act IV., Sc. 4.

Of stone worship there are still many vestiges. In a little island near Skye is a chapel dedicated to St. Columbus; on an altar is a round blue stone which is always moist. Fishermen, detained by contrary winds, bathe this stone in water, expecting thereby to obtain favorable winds; it is likewise applied to the sides of people troubled with stitches, and it is held so holy, that decisive oaths are sworn upon it.

There is a stone in the parish of Madren, Cornwall, through which many persons are wont to creep for pains in the back and limbs, and through which children are drawn for the rickets. In the North, children are drawn through a hole cut in the *Groaning Cheese*, a huge stone, on the day they are christened.

To go into the cleft of a rock was an ancient method of penitence and purification. It may be remembered that in the tradition of Hiram Abiff, the assassins were found concealed in a hollow rock, in which they were lamenting their crime.

To sleep on stones on particular nights is a cure for lameness with our peasants, though perhaps a hazardous one, especially if the disease originated from rheumatism.

A Druidic monument of great historical interest is to be seen under the coronation chair in Westminster Abbey. Originally called *Liag-fial*, the Fatal Stone, by others *Cloch na cineamhna* or the Stone of Fortune, it was that upon which the Kings of Ireland used to be inaugurated, and which, being enclosed in a wooden chair, was, by the ingenuity of the Druids, made to emit a sound under the rightful candidate, and mute under a man of bad title. It was superstitiously sent to confirm the Irish colony in Scotland, and it continued at Scone as the coronation of the Scotch Kings, from the commencement of the Christian Era till 1300 A. D., when Edward I.

imported it into England. It is still a superstition in the Highlands that those who lay their hands against the Druids' stones will not prosper.

Many of these monuments are approached with great reverence by the natives of Scotland and the Isles, especially the *Tighte nan Druidhneach* in the Isle of Skye, little arched, round stone buildings capable of holding one, where the contemplative Druid sat when his oak could not shelter him from the weather. The common people never pass these without walking round them three times from east to west.

In Chartres, which teems with Druidic vestiges, a curious specimen of stone worship remains. At the close of service in the cathedral, no one leaves the church without kneeling and saying a short prayer before a small pillar or stone—without polish, base or capital—placed in a niche, and much worn on one side by the kisses of the devout. This stone is rumored to be of high antiquity, even earlier than the establishment of Christianity—for many centuries to have remained in a crypt of the cathedral where lamps were constantly burning—but the stairs having been much worn on one side by the great resort of pilgrims to the spot, the stone had been removed from its original site, to avoid the expenses of repairs. It was said to be a miraculous stone, and that its miracles were performed at the intercession of the Virgin Mary.

There is a certain reverence paid by the peasantry to those caves in which the Druids held their initiatory rites. Many of them are said to be inhabited by spirits, and there is one in the neighborhood of Dunskey, Scotland, which is held in peculiar veneration. At the change of the moon it is usual to bring even from a great distance infirm persons, and particularly rickety children whom they supposed bewitched, to bathe in a stream which flows from the hill, and then to dry them in the cave.

As among the Druids it is still customary to place a platter of salt and earth upon the breast of the corpse in many parts of Britain. Salt was held in great reverence by the Eastern nations as an emblem of incorruptibility. So among us to spill salt is considered unlucky; it was only the other day that I saw a talented and well educated lady overwhelmed with consternation at this mishap, but with admirable presence of mind she flung a pinch over her left shoulder and so recovered her self-possession.

Hare was forbidden to the ancient Britons by their religion, and to this day the Cornish eat it with reluctance. Boadicea also augured from the running of a hare; and a hare that runs across a path (to any

one but a sportsman, or rather a pot-hunter) is an
omen of ill-luck.

The onion was an emblem of the deity among the
Egyptians, perhaps also among the Druids, for it is
a custom in some parts of England for girls to divine
by it, as Barnaby Googe in his translation of Naogeorgus' Popish Kingdome informs us.

In these same days young wanton gyrles that meete for marriage be,
Doe search to know the names of them that shall their husbands bee;
Four onyons, five, or eight, they take, and make in every one
Such names as they do fancie most, and best to think upon,
Thus nere the chimney them they set, and that same Onyon then
That firste doth sproute, doth surely bear the name of their good man.

In matters of dress, there are not many traces of
the Druids and the ancient Britons to be found.

The caps of rushes, however, which they wore
tied at the top and twisted into a band at the bottom, may still be seen upon the heads of children in
Wales and some parts of England.　In Shetland, the
ancient sandals of untanned skins are worn, and
also, by fishermen in cold weather, the Druidic
wooden shoes.　I could not discover their real origin
during my visit there: some said they had been
imported by the Dutch, others that the Dutch had
borrowed the idea from them; but in any case these
wooden shoes, the *sabots* of the lower orders of
France, are derived from the Druids.

The best instance of dress however, is the Highland plaid, which was the very garment worn by the

Druid Abaris, on his visit to Athens, and which is an extraordinary example of savage conservatism. From the *breachan* of the Gauls and Britons, is derived our word *breeches* and also that inelegant but necessary article of clothing.

Upon the subject of words I will also remark that our word *fortnight* or fourteen nights, is derived from the Druidic habit of counting time by nights instead of days; and the word *dizzy* from their *deisul*, or circular dance, (in Hebrew *dizzel*). I could give a multitude more, but *ohe! jam satis est.*

A very curious memorial of Druidism in the very bosom of victorious Christianity was discovered a few years ago by the well-known French Antiquary, M. Hersart de la Villemarqué. It is a fragment of Latin poetry which all the children in the parish of Nizon, Canton de Pont-Aven, are taught to sing at school and in church. The original poetry is almost the same as its Latin adaptation, except that in the latter various biblical allusions have been slipped in.

I will give the first strophe of the original, then its translation in the French of M. Villemarqué which is too good for me to meddle with, and then the Latin hymn as sung by the children :—

ANN DROUIZ.

Daik mab gwenn Drouiz; ore;
Daik petra fell d'id-dei
Petra ganinn-me d'id-de.

AR MAP

Kan d'in euz a eur raun,
Ken a ouffenn breman.

LE DRUIDE.

Tout beau enfant blanc du Druide, tout beau réponds-moi; que veux-tu? te chanterai-je?

L'ENFANT.

Chante-moi la division du nombre un jusqu'à ce que je l'apprenne aujourd'hui.

LE DRUIDE.

Pas de division pour le nombre un, la nécessitéuni que; la mort père de la douleur; rien avant, rien après. Tout beau, &c.

L'ENFANT.

Chante-moi la division du nombre deux, &c.

LE DRUIDE.

Deux bœufs attelés à une coque; ils tirent, ils vont expirer—Voyez la merveille !
Pas de division, &c.

L'ENFANT.

Chante-moi la division du nombre trois, &c.

LE DRUIDE.

Il y a trois parties dans le monde; trois commencements et trois fins pour l'homme, comme pour le chêne; trois célestes royaumes de Merlin; fruits d'or, fleurs brillantes, petits enfants qui rient.
Deux bœufs, &c.
Pas de division, &e.

The christianized version in Latin is as follows:

L'ENFANT.

Dic mihi quid unus,
Dic mihi quid unus.

LE MAITRE.

Unus est Deus,
Qui regnat in Cœlis.

L'ENFANT.

Dic mihi quid duo.
Dic mihi quid duo.

LE MAITRE.
Duo testamenta,
Unus est Deus,
Qui regnat in Cœlis.

L'ENFANT.
Dic mihi qui sunt tres
Dic mihi que sunt tres.

LE MAITRE.
Tres sunt patriarchæ,
Duo sunt testamenta;
Unus est deus,
Qui regnat in Cœlis.

Both of these dialogues are continued to the number twelve. In the Druidic version containing precepts on theology, cosmogony, chronology, astronomy, geography, magic, medicine and history. The Latin version teaching that there is one God, two testaments, three prophets, four evangelists, five books of Moses, six pitchers at the marriage of Cana, seven sacraments, eight beatitudes, nine choirs of angels, ten commandments, eleven stars which appeared to Joseph, and twelve apostles.

The resemblance of style and precept throughout is very striking, and a discovery which I have made of the same nature renders it still more surprising.

There is a peculiar song of the Oxfordshire peasants, the meaning of which had often perplexed me and which of course those who sung it were the least able to explain.

It is sung in this manner. One of them begins:—

I will sing you my one O !

To which the rest sing in chorus.

What is your one O !

And he sings.

One is all alone,
And ever doth remain so.

The song continues to the number twelve, each verse repeated after each as in the original versions above.　Most of these verses are local corruptions, and it is probable that in some parts of England a purer version is retained.　However, since the first refers to the One Deity, the second to "two white boys clothed in green," the fourth to "four gospel preachers," the seventh to the "seven stars," &c., there can be no doubt as to its origin.

There is so superstitious a reverence paid by the lower orders in many parts of Britain to bees, that one is almost inclined to suppose that they also were held sacred by the Druids.

The Cornishmen consider bees too sacred to be bought.　In other counties, on the death of their proprietor, a ceremonious announcement of the fact is made to them and a piece of funeral cake presented to them.　It is believed that were this omitted they would fly away.　In Lithuania a similar practice prevails.

There is no clue to this, except in the circumstance that *the bee-hive* is one of the emblems of Freemasonry, and like many other Druidic and Masonic symbols, *e. g.* the seven stars, the cross-keys, &c., a favorite tavern sign. For instance the one at Abingdon, under which is written the following jocose distich:

> Within this hive were all alive,
> Good liquor makes us funny,
> So if your dry, come in and try,
> The flavor of our honey.

From the apple-tree the Druids were wont to cut their divining rods. And to this tree at Christmas, in Devon, Cornwall and other counties a curious ceremony is paid. The farmer and his laborers soak cakes in cider, and place them on the trenches of an apple tree, and sprinkling the tree repeat the following incantation :

> Here's to thee, old apple tree !
> Whence thou mayst bud, and whence thou mayest blow.
> Hats full ! Caps full ?
> Bushel, bushel, sacks full !
> And my pockets full too ! Huzza !

After which they dance round the tree and get drunk on the cider which remains. They believe that if they did not do this the tree would not bear.

I have now to consider the vestiges of mistletoe-worship extant among the descendants of the Druids.

On Christmas Eve it was lately the custom at York to carry mistletoe to the high altar of the Cathedral, and to proclaim a public and universal liberty, pardon and freedom to all sorts of inferior and even wicked people at the gates of the city towards the four quarters of heaven.

The mistletoe was considered of great medicinal virtue by Sir John Coldbatch for epilepsy and other convulsive disorders. The mistletoe of the oak is used by the common people for wind ruptures in children.

Like the *houzza !* of the East, the mistletoe would seem to have a religious exclamation, as I judge from finding it so often the refrain to old French songs, especially this one :

O gué la bonne adventure, O gué.

And in one celebrated English ballad :

O the mistletoe bough ! and O the mistletoe bough !

It is still a custom in many parts of France for children to run down the street on New Year's Day, and to rap the doors crying " *Au gui l'an né*, or *Au gui, l'an neuf.*"

In the island of Sein, there is a mistletoe feast which it is believed has been perpetuated by the Bas Breton *tailors* who, strange to say, have been formed from time immemorial into a fine association. They are poets, musicians and wizards who never contract marriages with strangers, and who have a language of their own, called *lueache* which they will not speak in the presence of foreigners.

At this feast there is a procession. An altar covered with green boughs is erected in the centre of a circular space of ground. Thence they start, and thither marching round the island return. Two fiddlers form the vanguard; they are followed by children carrying bill-hooks and oak-branches, and leading an ox and a horse covered with flowers. After them a huge crowd which stops at intervals crying *Gui-na-né voilà le Gui.*

There is one more mistletoe custom which I had almost forgotten. Let us imagine ourselves in the hall of some old-fashioned country mansion. Let it be Christmas-night, and at that hour when merriment and wine has flushed every face, and glowed into every heart.

And now I will paint to you a young maiden who embraced in the arms of her lover is whirled round the hall, her eyes sparkling, her white bosom heaving and her little feet scarce seeming to touch the floor. They pause for a moment. An old lady with an arch twinkle in her eye whispers something to her partner, he nods and smiles; she blushes and turns her eyes, pretending not to hear.

They join the dance again, when suddenly he stays her in the centre of the hall. Above their heads droops down a beautiful plant with pale white berries and leaves of a delicate green. He stoops and gives her *the kiss-under-the-mistletoe.* All laugh and follow his example till the scene vies the revels of the ancient Bacchanals.

It is this picture which awakes me from a reverie into which I have long been buried. Reader! you have sought with me for the first germs of religion in the chaos of youthful Time; you have dived with me into those mysteries which the Veil of Isis held secret from our sight; you have sojourned with me among the tombs of the past, and trod upon the dust of a fallen World.

Let us now return from these caverns of learning to the glorious day-light of the Present, and to the enjoyments of a real existence.

APPENDIX.

APPENDIX.

Instead of disfiguring the pages of this volume with marginal references, which no one examines, and with footnotes, which scarcely any one reads, I have prepared a catalogue of the works consulted upon the subjects of Paganism, the Druids, the early Britons, the Roman Catholics, the Freemasons, and the Folk-lore of our peasants, as discussed in this work, and which, though an imperfect one, is sufficient as a pledge of my industry and good faith, and as a guide to those who may feel inclined to illumine with their stronger lights that upon which I have but thrown the faint glimmer of a green torch.

Catalogue of Works consulted for the Veil of Isis.

Aberffraw Royal Eistedfodd, Transactions of.
Acta Sanctorum, ou Chronologie de l'Historie de la Franche-Maçonnerie.
Adam's Letters on the Masonic Institution.
Adam's Religious World Displayed.
Ælian, De Natura Animalium.
Agathemeri, Geographiæ Expositionum.
Aglio, Antiquities of Mexico.

Allen's Modern Judaism.
Alley's Vindiciæ Christianæ.
Alphonso Liguori, Glories of Mary.
Ambrosii, Opera.
Annales Cambriæ.
Anselm, Liber de excellentiâ gloriosæ Virginis Mariie.
Ansted's Ancient World.
Antonini Itinerarium.
Anthologia Græca e recensione Brunckii.
Appiani, Historia.

Appleyard's Welsh Sketches.
Appolonii Alexandrini, Opera.
Archæologia Cambrensis.
Arcq, Histoire de Commerce.
Argentré, Historie de Bretagne.
Aristides, Orationes.
Aristotellis Opera.
Ashe, Masonic Manuel.
Asiatic Researches.
Asplin's Alkibla, or, Disquisitions on Worshipping towards the East.
Astle, on Stone Pillars, Crosses, and Crucifixes.
Astle's Origin and Progress of Writing.
Athanasii Opera.
Athenæi Deipnosophistæ.
Avienii Fragmenta.
Ausonii Epigrammata.
Authentic History of Free-masonry.
Auvergne, Account of an Historical Monument in Brittany.

Bacon's Reliques of Rome.
Bailey's Rituale Catholicum.
Baillet, De la Dévotion á la Sainte Vierge.
Bailli, De la Grande Bretagne Armorique.
Baldwin's (Archbishop), Itinerary through Wales.
Banier, Mythology.
Barlow's Adoration of the Cross.
Barrington's Observations upon the Statutes.
Basilii Opera.
Baur, Symbolik und Mythologie.
Baxter's Glossarium Antiquitatum Britannicarum.
Beaudieu, Mémoire à consulter pour les Anciens Druides.
Beaufort, Légendes et Traditiones populaires de la France.
Bedœ, Historia Ecclesiastica.
Beke's Origines Biblicæ.
Benedictus XIV., Works of
Bentham, The Gael and Cimbri.
Berosus et Manetho apud Ensebium.
Beugnot, Histoire de la destruction du Paganisme en Occident.
Bingham's Christian Antiquities.
Bingley's Tour in North Wales.

Blasio. Thesaurus Antiquitatum Sacrarum.
Blunt's Vestiges of Ancient Customs and Manners in Modern Italy and Sicily.
Bobrick's Gerschichte der Freimaurerey.
Bolliger, Ideen zur Kunst Mythologie.
Bonnechose, L es Quatres Conquêtes de l'Angleterre.
Bonnelier, Les Vieilles Femmes d I'lle de Sein.
Borelius, Trésor des Recherches et Antiquités Gauloises.
Borlase, Natural History of Cornwall.
Borlase, Antiquities of Cornwall.
Boullanger, L'Antiquité Devoilèe.
Boullanger, Le Christianisme Devoilée.
Boullanger, De la Cruauté Religieuse·
Bourgneville, Recherches et Antiquités de la Province de Neustrie.
Bourne's Antiquitates Vulgares.
Bowles, Hermes Britannicus.
Brand's History of Newcastle.
Brand's Observations on Popular Antiquities.
Bretagne, Les Coustumes du pays.
Brewer's Picture of England.
Brewer's Beauties of England and Wales.
British Apollo (The)
Broughton's Dictionary of all Religions.
Browne's History of the Highlands and Highland clans.
Brugsch Inscriptio Rosettana Hieroglyphica.
Brunel, Avant le Christianisme.
Brut Y., Tywysogion.
Buat, Histoire des Anciens Peuples d'Europe.
Buat, Les Origines.
Buck's Theological Dictionary.
Buck's View of Antiquities in Wales.
Buckland's Reliquiæ Diluvianiæ.
Burder's Account of the Idolatry of Pagan Nations.

Burder's Oriental Customs
Burton's History of Wales.
Bush's Hibernia Curiosa.
Busk's Manners and Customs of the Japanese.
Buttmann's Mythologus.

Cæsaris Commentari.
Caledonion Bards, Works of, translated from the Gaelic.
Calfhille's Answere to the Treatise of the Crosse.
Calmet, de la Poésie et Musique des Anciens Hébreux.
Calmet, Dictionnaire de la Bible.
Cambrian Popular Antiquities.
Cambro-Briton and General Celtic Repository.
Cambry, Monumens Celtiques.
Camden's Britannia.
Campion's History of Ireland.
Capefigue, Histoire Philosophique des Juifs.
Capitolini Orationes.
Carew's Survey of Cornwall.
Cat out of the Bag, containing the whole Secrets of the Mysteries of Freemasonry.
Catulli Carmina.
Caumont, Cours d'Antiquitiés Monumentales.
Caumont, Abrécedaire, ou Rudiment d'Archéologie.
Cawdy, Concerning Superstition, with Worship, and Christmas Festival.
Cellarii, Notitia Orbis Antiqui.
Centinela contra Frans-masones.
Chalmer's Caledonia.
Chamyollion, Le Jeune Précis du Systéme Hiéroglyphique des Anciens Egyptiens.
Chastel, Histoire de la Destruction du Paganisme dans l'Empire d'Orient.
Chauncey's History and Antiquities of Hertfordshire.
Chorier, Histoire de Dauphiné.
Chrysostomi Opera.
Churchill, Divi Britannici,
Churchyard's Worthies of Wales.
Ciceronis Opera.
Clagnet, Concerning the Invocation of the Saints and the Virgin Mary.

Clavel, L'histoire pittoresque de la franc-maçonnerie.
Cleland's Specimens of an Etymological Vocabulary.
Cleland's Essay on the Real Secrets of Freemasonry.
Cligetoveus, De puritate conceptionis benedictæ Mariæ Virginis.
Coate's History of Reading.
Collection of Letters on Freemasonry.
Collinson's Beauties of England.
Conder, View of all Religions.
Confucius, traduit par Gaubil.
Constitutions of the Freemasons.
Cook's Inquiry into the Patriarchal and Druidical Religions.
Corrozet, Les Antiquitez Croniques et singularitez de Paris.
Cory's Fragments.
Cory's Mythological Inquiry into Heathen recondite Theology.
Cory's Metaphysical Inquiry into Ancient and Modern Philosophy.
Courson, Histoire des Origines et des Institutions des Peuples de la Gaule Armoricaine.
Courson, Histoire des Peuples Bretons.
Crantz, History of Greenland.
Crawfurd's Researches.
Cressy's Church History.
Creuzer, Symbolik und Mythologie.
Cumberland's Origines Gentes Antiquissimæ.
Cuvier, Researches sur les Ossements Fossiles des Quadrupédes.
Cymmroddion, or Metropolitan Cambrian Society, Transactions of.

Dafenbach, Celtica Sprachliche Documente zur Geschichte der Kelten.
Dale, Dissertationes de Origine ac Progressu Idolatriæ.
Dalrymple, Disquisitions concerning the Antiquities of the Christian Church.
Daniel, Thesaurus Hymnologicus.

Daniel, Codex Liturgicus.
Daru, Histoire de Bretagne.
Davis, Ancient Rites and Monuments of the Monastical and Cathedral Church of Durham.
Davies, Dictionarium Antiquæ Linguæ Britannicæ.
Davies, Welsh Botanology.
Davies, Celtic Researches.
Davies, Rites and Ceremonies of the Druids.
Davies, Cambro-Britannicæ Cymraecœve Linguæ Institutiones et Rudimenta.
Deane's Worship of the Serpent.
De la Rue. Essias Historiques sur les Bardes.
Delaune's Plea for Nonconformists.
Der Friedenker in der Maurerei.
Der Freimaurer orden in seiner Nichtigkeit.
De Rossi, Bibliotheca Judaica et Anti-Christiana.
Développement des abus introduits dans la Franc-maconnerie.
Dictionnaire Historique des cultes Religieux.
Didon, Histoire Sainte.
Diez, Leben und Werke der Troubadours.
Diodori Siculi Opera.
Dioscoridis, Historia.
Dodridge's Account of the Principality of Wales.
Dorothœi Synopsis Varium Historiarum.
Druids, Complete History of
Druid's Magazine.
Druidess (the), a Tale, translated from the German.
Duchesne, Historiæ Normanorum Scriptores Antiqui.
Duclos, Mémores sur les Druides.
Du Halde's History of China.
Dulaure, Cultes qui out précédé et amené l'Idolatrie ou l'Adoration des Figures Humaines.
Dupuis, Origine de tous les cults.
Dupuis, Analyse raisonnée de l'Origine de tous les Cultes.

Early History of the Cymry.
Eastcott, Sketches of the Origin. Progress and Effects of Music.

Eccleston's Introduction to English Antiquities.
Encyclopœdia of Religious Knowledge.
Enderbie's Cambria Triumphans.
Enoch, Le Vrai Franc-maçon.
Ernstin's Ad Antiquitates Etruscas.
Esprit du Dogme de la Franche-Maçonnerie.
Essex, On Origin and Antiquity of Round Churches.
Estienne, Apologie pour Herodote.
Etymologicium Magnum Sylburgii.
Eusebii Opera.
Evan's Specimens of the Poetry of the Ancient Welsh Bards.
Evan's British Herbal.
Evan's Gwinlanny Bardd sef Pryddwaith ar Cymryive destunau a Gwahanol Fesurau.
Evan's Tour in South Wales.
Evan's Dissertatio de Bardis.
Evelyn's Sibra.
Ewald, Briefe uber d'alte Mystik und den neuen Mysticismus.
Explanation of the Masonic Plate.

Faber's Mysteries of the Cabiri.
Faber's Origin of Pagan Idolatry.
Fairholt's Costume in England.
Fane of the Druids. A Poem.
Farrar's Ecclesiastical Dictionary.
Fauchet, Les Antiquitéz Gauloises.
Fellow's Exposition of the Mysterious Dogmas of the Ancient Egyptians.
Firmicus, de Errore profanarum Religionum.
Fleury, Mœurs des Israélites et des Chrétiens.
Fontenelie, Histoire des Oracles.
Forster's One Primeval Language.
Fosbrohe's Encyclopædia of Antiquities.
Foster's Sketches of the Mythology of the Hindoos.
Fouqué's, Sir Elidoc, an old Breton Legend.

Appendix.

Foye's Romish Rites, Offices, and Legends.

Francs-Macons, leurs Devoirs, Statuts, ou Réglements généraux.

Freeman, on Great and Good Effects of the Universal Medicine of the Magi.

Freemasons (the), an Hudibrastick Poem.

Freemasonry, its Pretensions Exposed.

Freemasonry in Europe during the Past Century.

Freemason's Occupation and Defense in Six Letters

Freret, Académe des Inscriptions.

Froissart, Chroniques de

Fuller's Church History.

Gallicarum et Francicarum rerum Scriptores.

Grennadius De Illustribus Ecclesiæ Scriptoribus.

Gerhard, Archæolog-Zeitung.

Getty's Notices of Chinese Seals found in Ireland.

Gildæ Sapientis de Excidio Britanniæ.

Giraldi Cambrensis, Expugnatio Hiberniæ.

Giraldi Cambrensis, Topographia Hibernica.

Giraldi Cambrensis, Itinerarium Cambriæ.

Giraldi Cambrensis, Itinarium Cambrine.

Gliddon's Otia Egyptiaca.

Good's Description of Manners and Customs of the Wild Irish.

Grævius Thesaurus Antiqualitium Romanarum.

Grant's Superstitions of the Highlanders.

Grave's History of Cleveland.

Grimm, Deutsche Mythologie.

Grove's Antiquities of Ireland.

Grose's View of Antiquities of Wales.

Grose's Provincial Glossary.

Guenebault Dictionnaire Incono-grapeique des Monuments de l'Antiquité Chrétienne.

Guerin du Rocher, Histoire véritable des Temps fabuleux.

Guest (Lady Charlotte), Mabinogion.

Guthrie, Dissertation sur les Antiquités de Russie.

Hakewell's Antiquity of Christian Religion in Britain.

Hale's History of the Jews.

Halliwell's Early History of Freemasonry in England.

Hall's Triumphs of Rome.

Hammer's History of Ireland.

Hammer, Mémore sur la culte de Mithra.

Hardiman's Irish Minstrelsy.

Hasted's History of Kent.

Hawkin's History of Music.

Hall's Chronicle of England.

Hammer's History of Ireland.

Heeren's Historical Researches.

Heggesippi Opera.

Henry's History of England.

Henry, l'Egypte Pharonique.

Henry, Histoire du Christianisme.

Herbert's Britannia after the Romans.

Herbert's Britannia Sancta.

Herbert's Cyclops Christianus.

Herbert's Essay on the Neo-Druidists.

Herodianus.

Herodotis, Historiæ.

Heroic Elegies of Llywarch Hen.

Herrick's Hesperides.

Hervart, De Antiquissima Veterum Nationium Superstitione.

Higden's Polychronicon.

History of Anglesey.

Histoirie of Great Britaine.

Hoech, Veteris Mediæ et Persiæ Monumenta.

Holwell's Mythological Dictionary.

Hollwell's Fasts and Festivals of the Hindoos.

Hope's Costume of the Ancients.

Horatii Opera.

Horsley's Britannia Romana.

Howel, Ancient Laws and Institutes of Wales.

Holinshed's Chronicles of England, Ireland, and Scotland.

Hughes Horæ Britannicæ.

Humboldt's Researches on Ancient Inhabitants of America.
Hurd's Rites and Ceremonies of the Whole World.
Hutchinson's History of Cumberland.
Husbandman's Practice and Prognostication for Ever.
Hyde, Veterum Persarum Parthorium et Medorum Religionis Historia.

I. T., Collection of Welsh Travels.
Identity of Religions called Hebrew and Druidic.
Inne's Critical Essay on Ancient Inhabitants of Scotland.
Institutio Archœol. Monument, Antichi, Inediti.
Instructions des Trois premier. Grades de la Franche-Maconnerie.
Introduction to Freemasonry.
Iolo, Manuscripts, Selection of Ancient Welsh MSS.
Ionian Antiquities, by Chandler Revelt and Pars.
Isidori, Hispalensis Episcopi Opera.

Jablonski, Pantheon Ægyptiorum.
Jablonski, Opuscula.
Jackson's Chronological Antiquities.
Jacquemin le Franc-maçon.
Jacquin et Duesberg, Dictionnaire d'Antiquités Chrétiennes.
Jamblicus de Mysteriis.
Jamblicus de Vitâ Pythagorica.
James, Patriarchal Religion of Britain.
Jamieson, History of the Culdees.
Jenning's Jewish Antiquities.
Johnstone's Antiquitates Celto-normanicæ.
Johnstone's Antiquitates Celto-Scandicæ.
Jones' Bardic Museum of Primitive British Literature.
Jone's History of Wales.
Jones' Musical and Poetical Relicks of the Welsh Bards.

Jones' Scripture Antiquities.
Jones' Illustrations of the National History of the Snowdonian Mountains.
Jones' Stonehenge Restored.
Jormandez, De Getarûm sive Gothorum Origine.
Josephi, Antiquitates et Bellum Judaicum.
Juvenalis Satyræ.

Kaufmann et Cherpin Histoire Philosophique de la Franc-maçonnerie.
Keightley's Mythology of Greece and Italy.
Kenrick's Ancient Egypt under the Pharoahs.
Kenrick's Phenica.
Ker's Archæology of our popular Phrases.
Keyser's Religion of Northmen, trans.
Keyser, De Deâ Nehalenniâ.
Keysler, Antiquitates Selectæ Septentrionales.
Keysler, de culta Solis.
Kidd's China.
King, Rites and Ceremonies of the Greek Church in Russia.
Knight's Inquiry into the Symbolical Language of Ancient Art and Mythology.
Knight, on the Worship of Priapus.
Krasinki, Lectures on Religious History of Sclavonic Nations.
Kruase, die Drei altesten Kunslurkunden der deutschen Freimaurer Bruderschaft.

Lacombe, Dictionnaire du vieux Langage François.
Lafitau, Mœurs des Sauvages Américaines.
Landon, Ecclesiastical Dictionnaire.
Lane's Egyptian Antiquities.
Lasteyrie, History of Auricular Confession.
Latour-d'Auvergne Corret, Origines Gauloises.
Layamon's Brût or Chronicle of Britain.

Mayo's Mythology.
Melæ Pomponii, Opera.
Mémoires de la Société Royale des Antiquaires du Nord.
Méril, Mélanges Archéologiques et Littéraires.
Messe (la) et ses Mystéres, comparés aux Mystères Anciens.
Migne, Encyclopédie Théologique.
Millin, Galérie Mythologique.
Milman's History of Christianity.
Milner's Inquiry into certain Vulgar Opinions respecting the Catholic Inhabitants of Ireland.
Minucii Felicis, Opera.
Mischna, sive totius Hebræorum Juris Rituium Antiquitatum ac Legum Oratium Systema.
Missale Romanum.
Misson, Travels in England (translated).
Moke, Mœurs, Usuages, Fêtes, et Solemnités des Belges.
Montiers, Le Sommaire des Antiquitez et Merveilles d'Ecose.
Moore's History of Devonshire.
Moore's History of Ireland.
Morice, Preuves de l'Histoire de Bretagne.
Morini, Antiquitates Ecclesiæ Orientalis.
Morison's Religious History of Man.
Moroni, Dizionario Ecclesiastico.
Motherwell's Minstrelsy, Ancient and Modern.
Muratori, Novus Thesaurus Veterum Inscriptionum.
Murtadi, History of the Pyramids of Egypt.
Musgrave, Antiquitates Britanno-Belgicœ.
Mussard's Conformity between Ancient and Modern Ceremonies.
Myrvyrian, Archæology of Wales.

Naogeorgus' Popish Kingdome.
Neercassel, on Worship of the Saints and the Virgin.
Nemesiani, Eclogæ.
Nennii, Eulogium Britanniæ.
Nibbi, Elementi di Archeologiæ.

Nimrod's Discourse upon certain passages in History and Fable.
Nolten's Conspectus Thesauri Antiquitatum Germanicarum.
Northern Antiquities, by Sir W. Scott, H. Weber, and R. Jamieson.
Nouveau Catéchisme des Francmacon.

O'Brien's Round Towers of Ireland.
Œltinger, Archives, Historiques.
O'Flaherty's Ogygia.
O'Halloran's History of Ireland.
Oliver's Star of Glory.
Oliver's Theocratic Philosophy of Freemasonry.
Oliver's Jacob's Ladder.
Oliver's Institutes of Masonic Jurisprudence.
Oliver's Insignia of the Royal Arch.
Oliver's Mirror for the Johanuite Masons.
Oliver's Revelations of a Square.
Oliver's History of Freemasonry.
Oliver's Existing Remains of Ancient Britons.
Oliver's Book of the Lodge.
Oliver's Star in the East.
Oliver's History of Initiation.
Oliver's Antiquities of Freemasonry.
Oliver's Dictionary of Symbolic Masonry.
Oliver's Golden Remains of the Early Masonic Writers.
Oliver's Signs and Symbols, illustrated and explained.
Oliver's Historical Land-Marks of Freemasonry.
Oppiani Halieutica.
L'Orateur Franc-maçon.
L'Ordre des Francs-maçons.
Origenis Opera.
Orme's History of England.
Orosii Historæ.
Orphei Argonautica.
Osborne's Advice to his Son.
Osborne's Antiquities of Egypt.
Ossianic Society, Transactions of.
Ovidii Opera.
Owen's British Remains.

Owen's History of Consecration of Altars and Churches.

P * * * (Madame de), Recherches Philosophiques sur les Egyptiens et les Chinois.

Paciaudi, Treatise on Ancient Crosses found at Ravenna.

Palmer's Origines Liturgicæ.

Pamphili Chronica.

Parfait Maçon (le).

Parkinson's Collectanea, Anglo-Minoritica.

Parson's Remains of Japhet.

Pasquier, Recherches de la France.

Pauthier, Essai sur l'origine et la formation similaire des écritures Egyptiens et Chinois.

Pauw, Recherches Philosophiques sur les Américains.

Pauzer, Beitrag zur Deutschen Mythologie.

Pechey, Upon the Serpent Stones imported from the East Indies.

Pelloutier, Histoire des Celtes.

Percy's Reliques of Ancient Minstrelsy.

Peirie's Round Towers of Ireland.

Peyrat, Histoire et Religion.

Philosophy of Masons.

Pictet, De l'Affinité de Langues Celtes avec le Sanscrit.

Pictet, La Mystère des Bardes de l'Ile de Bretagne.

Pièces mêlées paur sevir à l'Histoire de la Maçonnerie.

Piper, Mythologie und Symbolik.

Pitre (Chevalier), Bretagne, Ancienns et Moderne.

Plinii, Historia Naturalis.

Plot's Natural History of Oxfordshire.

Plot's Natural History of Staffordshire.

Plutarchi Opera.

Polenus, Miscellanea Eruditæ Antiquitatis.

Polwhele's History of Cornwall.

Polwhele's History of Devonshire.

Polwhele's Language and Literature of Cornwall.

Polybii Opera.

Poole's Horæ Egyptiacæ.

Portal, Coleurs Symboliques dans l'Antiquité.

Portal, Symbols des Egyptiens comparées à ceux des Hébreux,

Postal, Couleurs Symboliques.

Poste's Britannic Researches.

Powel's Historia of Cambria.

Price's Historiæ Britannicæ Defensio.

Prichard's Analysis of Egyptian Mythology.

Prichard's Eastern Origin of the Celtic Nations.

Prichard's Songs of the Aboriginal Bards of Britain.

Prideaux' Connections.

Proscopini Opera.

Prosperi Aquitani Opera.

Ptolomæi Geographia Bertii.

Pugin, Glossary of Ecclesiastical Ornament and Costume.

Quatremére, Mémoires Géographiques et Historiques sur l'Egypte.

Quintillianis Institutiones Orationæ.

Quinet, Génie des Religions.

R. B. History of Wales.

Rafn, Antiquités Américaines.

Rammohun Roy's Translation of the Vedas.

Rangabe, Antiquités Helléniques.

Rawlinson's Cruciform Inscriptions of Babylon and Assyria.

Rebold, Histoire génerale de la Franc-Maçonneri.

Recherches Philosophiques sur les Américaines.

Recherches Philosophiques sur les Egyptiens.

Ree's Essay on the Welch Saints.

Richard f Circencester, Description of Britain.

Riddle's Manual of Christian Antiquities.

Ridpath's Border History.

Rimbault's Old Songs and Ballard's.

Rock's Hærugia.

Robert's Sketch of the Early History of the Cymry.

Robert's Early History of the Britons.
Robert's Chronicle of Kings of Britain.
Robert's Cambrian Popular Antiquities.
R o b i n, Mont-Glonn, ou R e-cherches Historiques sur l'origines des Celtes.
Robinson's Theological Dictionary.
Robison's Proofs (*Masonic.*)
Rollin, Histoire Ancienne.
Rutillii Opera.

Sacrifices, An Essay on the Origin and Design of.
Sacy, Histoire des Institutions de Moise.
Sanchoniatho's Phenician History, (*translated by Bishop Cumberland.*)
Sale's Alcoran.
Savary, Lettres sur l'Egypte.
Saull's Nottia Britannica.
Samme's Britannia Antiqua Illustrata.
Schenkius on Images.
Schuleri Thesaurus Antiquitatium Teutonicarum.
Secret History of the Freemasons.
Secrets of the Freemasons revealed by a Disgusted Brother.
Sequestri Opera.
Seymour's Pilgrimage to Rome.
Shaw's History of Staffordshire.
Shaw, Concerning the Blessedness of the Virgin Mary.
Sidonii Opera.
Sinclair's Hill and Valley, and Wales and the Welsh.
Skene's Highlander's of Scotland.
Sloane, of the Pretended Serpent Stone.
Smith's Religion of the Ancient Britons.
Smith's Sacred Annals,
Smith's Gaelic Researches.
Smith's Sean Dana.
Souvestre, Les Derniers Bretons.
Sozomeni Opera.
Speed's History of Great Britain.

Spenser's View of the State of Ireland,
Squier's American Archœological Researches.
Stafford Ye Femal Glory.
Stanlhurst, De Rebus gestis in Hibernia.
Stephanii Opera.
Stephen's Literature of the Kymry.
Stillingfleet's Originas Sacræ.
Strabonis Geographia.
S t u k e l e y' s Stonehenge and Abury.
Stukeley's Itinerarium Curiosum.
Stukeley's Palæographic Britannica.
Stukeley's Palægraphia Sacra.
Stow's Chronicles of Britain.
Suetonii Tranquilli Opera.
Sulpitii Opera.
Symmachii Opera.

T. L., True Account of Britons by.
Taciti Historiæ.
Tavernier, Six Voyages en Turquie, Perse, et aux Indés.
Theodoreti Opera.
Thiers' Traité des Superstitions qui regardent les Sacrémens.
Thory, Acta Latomorum.
Thummel, Mexike und die Mexikaner.
Tibulli Opera.
Tod's Annals and Antiquities of Rajah'stan.
Toland's History of the Druids.
Trenchard's Natural History of Superstition.
Trimégiste, l'Art d'Expliquer les Songes.
Turner's Sacred History.
Turner's Vindication of the Genuineness of Ancient British Poems.
Tyler's Worship of the Virgin Mary.
Tyler's Primitive Christian Worship.

Valerii Opera.
Vallencey, Essay on Antiquity of Irish Languages.
Vallencey, On Ancient History of Britannic Isles.

Vallencey, Collectanea de Rebus Hibernicis.
Vaughan's British Antiquities.
Vaux, Ninevee and Persepolis.
Vegetii Opera.
Vernati, On the Medicinal Nature of Certain Stone found in the Indies in the Head of a Serpent.
Verstegan, Restitution of Decayed Intelligence in Antiquities.
Vertot, Historie Critique des Bretons.
Victoris, Opera.
Vergilii Æneis.
Vollstandige's Gesanbuch für Friemaurer.
Volney, Recherches Nouvelles sur l'Histoire Ancienne.
Volney, Les Ruines, &c.
Vopisci, Opera.

Wace, Le Roman de Brût.
Wachner, Antiquitates Hebrœorum et Israeliticæ Gentis.
Wachsmuth's Historical Antiquities of the Greeks.
Wakeman, Archæologia Hibernica.
Wallography, or Britons described.
Ware, de Hibernia.
Warner's Walk Through Wales.
Warrington's History of Wales.
Warton's History of English Poetry.
Webb's Antiquities of China.
Weever's Ancient Funeral Monuments of Great Britain.
Wellbeloved's Eburacum.

Welsh Traditions.
Werenfel's Superstition.
Whitaker's History of the Britons.
Whitaker's History of Manchester.
Whittington's Ecclesiastical Antiquities of France.
Wilhelmi Malmesburiensis Monachi, gesta rerum Anglorum.
William's Poems, Lyric and Pastoral.
William's History of Monmouthshire.
William's Dictionary of all Religions.
William's Masonry.
William's Ode on the British Druids.
William's Ecclesiastical Antiquities of the Cymry.
Wilson's Archæologica Dictionary.
Wilson's Nehustan.
Wilson's Vitis Degeneris; a treatise on Ancient Ceremonies.
Wilson's Vishnu Purana, or system of Hindu Mythology.
Worde Wynkyn (de), The Myracles of our Blessed Ladie.
Wotton's Rabinical Traditions.
Wotton's Leges Wallicæ.
Wright's Archælogical Album.
Wright's Celt, Roman and Saxon.
Wright's St. Patrick's Purgatory.
Wright's Louthiana.
Wyndham's Tour Through Wales.
Wynn's History of Wales,